sepia dreams

sepia

dreams

a celebration of black achievement
through words and images

**photographs and interviews by
matthew jordan smith**

written by dionne bennett with an
introduction by vanessa williams

st. martin's press ≋ new york

www.stmartins.com

Book design and composition by Victoria Kuskowski

ISBN 0-312-27817-9

First Edition: November 2001

10 9 8 7 6 5 4 3 2 1

for my loving parents,

mr. jordan smith &

mrs. eunice smith.

thank you for always

believing in me.

contents

sepia

(së′-pë-ə) 1. a dark-brown pigment.

2. a print or photograph of a brown color.

my sepia dream

My sepia dream began in a small town in South Carolina, and came true as a result of my own determination and the devotion of some incredible mentors. My most devoted mentor, and later my biggest fan, was my beloved preacher father. When I was twelve, he taught me how to use a camera and became my favorite partner in art when—to my sister's dismay—he turned our bathroom into a darkroom and taught me how to develop my own pictures. Knowing I was painfully shy, he showed me how the camera could become an extension of me, letting me reach people with images even when I couldn't reach them with words.

My other important mentors included the guidance counselor who told me to make a career out of photography, the photography professor who encouraged me to go to New York, the incredible photographers who trained me, and especially Susan L. Taylor, former editor-in-chief of *Essence* magazine. She gave me my first feature: hiring me to photograph Anita Hill at the height of the tumultuous Clarence Thomas confirmation hearings.

When I stepped out on my own to make my dreams come true, I found that the support I received from these mentors was indispensable. I have traveled all over the world as a photographer, but the longest, hardest trip of my life was from South Carolina to New York. I had no job and a place to stay for only two weeks. At that time, faith in my dream was my most valuable commodity, and in many ways it still is. Because I had a dream, I went from selling Armani ties at Bloomingdale's to photographing the models who wear them. Through faith in that dream I have turned dedication, determination, discipline, and a lot of old-fashioned hard work into a life that exceeds everything I thought possible.

As a child, when I first dreamed of becoming a professional photographer and looked for people whose lives and work could guide me, I searched for those who looked like me. Since there were no professional photographers living in my community, I turned to books. It took some searching, but eventually I found books on black photographers such as James Van Der Zee and Gordon Parks. Just the existence of those books—and those photographers—made my dreams seem possible.

Even those of us who have been lucky enough to have real-life mentors can benefit from the insight and inspiration of others—people we may not know personally, but whose lives can teach us lessons we need to learn. *Sepia Dreams* gives readers intimate advice from individuals who have served as role models to the entire world. It presents words of wisdom, accompanied by photographic portraits offered by fifty African-American superstars in the worlds of film, television, music, theater, dance, literature, fashion, and sports.

making *sepia dreams* come true

The title *Sepia Dreams* reflects my vision of a book devoted to photography, people of color, and dreams. Sepia is a tint used to describe a specific kind of photographic image. It can refer to a range of brown pigments, colors that remind me of the gorgeous hues of skin we see throughout the Black community—diverse shades of brown that are all equally beautiful and which are displayed in the images that fill the pages of this book. I decided to call my project *Sepia Dreams,* because the name, the images, and the words collectively symbolize a celebration of Black beauty and achievement.

Each photograph marks a memory of special moments I shared with each remarkable individual. During my photo session and interview with Lynn Whitfield, for example, she began crying and laughing. When I put my arms around her and asked her what was wrong, she told me that she had never done a photo shoot where she thought she looked so beautiful, and that she was so proud to see that the entire photo crew was African-American.

When Phylicia Rashad heard that I wanted to interview her, she called me personally to tell me that she "had to do my book" and invited me to the set of *Cosby* to interview her. She wept tears of joy at the end of the interview because she was so happy that young people would finally know what it takes to make it, instead of believing in the myth of overnight success.

When I first contacted Lena Horne, she graciously declined. However, I wrote her a personal letter telling her how many people had acknowledged that she inspired them. The next thing I knew Lena Horne herself called me and said, "Okay, dear, I'm ready to do your interview, let's go."

Back when *Sepia Dreams* was nothing more than a dream itself, I asked my friend Vanessa Williams to write the introduction to the book that I knew it would become. She agreed without hesitation and has remained a constant source of inspiration and encouragement. Photographing Vanessa with her husband, Rick Fox, only a month before she gave birth to their beautiful daughter reminded me of how far we had both come since I first photographed her in 1993. Every time I see her, I marvel along with everyone else at how one of the world's most beautiful women continues to grow even lovelier with each passing year. However, I am even more amazed at how this woman, whose dignity and determination defy every stereotype and every obstacle, has now turned her hard-won successes into well-deserved peace and joy that so vividly radiate from within her, making her one of my favorite photographic subjects. Sometimes I wonder if her courageous struggle is the secret behind her enduring beauty. Always, I know that the opportunity to witness, with my camera, her evolution as an artist and as a woman has been one of the great privileges of my career. Vanessa is a powerful living symbol of beauty, talent, and wisdom. She is everything that *Sepia Dreams* stands for.

Indeed, each celebrity tells a uniquely powerful story. Each celebrity's path to success is different, but their collective vision of a world in which we can all honor and share our gifts is the same. My dream is that this vision will light the way for readers like no other book has done before.

In speaking with countless people—both famous and familiar—about making their dreams come true, I've realized one thing above all. We as a people are not really moved by "silver platter" success stories. We are motivated by women and men who have cultivated the fruits of their labor with their bare hands and bold imaginations.

This is especially true of African-Americans, who have so often found themselves excluded both from the experiences of the so-called American Dream and from the images that claim to document it. We are rarely born with silver spoons in our mouths, and, despite what some ghetto-fabulous hip-hop videos would have us believe, African-Americans know that even the most successful among us never go from projects to penthouse in the time it takes to sign a contract and cut a record. We know that "living large" means working long and hard, and we know that the path to success is much bumpier and less direct than an easy walk down the plush red carpet of movie premiers and award shows. But many of us have trouble just finding the path, and those who *do* find it don't always know the best way to navigate it and stick to it until they reach their desired destination.

I decided to create *Sepia Dreams* because I wanted to help others make their dreams come true, just as I was helped by the mentors who loved, trained, and trusted me. *Sepia Dreams* presents to readers—in one package—the knowledge and inspiration that it took these fifty celebrities years to achieve for themselves. Most of us have to rely on faith and luck to make contact with people who possess the vital knowledge that we need to succeed. *Sepia Dreams* makes that connection for readers so that they can begin making their own dreams a reality.

I offer *Sepia Dreams* as a colorful map, a motivational model, a guided tour of success, and I hope that it will do for African-Americans what those early books about Black photographers did for me. Together, the words and images allow the reader to experience the power of each celebrity's physical presence as well as their professional and spiritual knowledge. Through *Sepia Dreams,* people who have lost sight of their vision—or who have yet to find it—will see success in living color, hold it in their hands, and believe that it is possible for them, just as it was for the incredible people who contributed to this book. It is my deepest hope that, after reading *Sepia Dreams,* those readers who have been tempted to surrender their own dreams will be convinced instead to reclaim them and to be guided by the stories' wisdoms. Those who do will find that hopefulness—which is too often discredited as a luxury of the young, foolish, and privileged—is a form of power to which we all have access, a power that gives dignity and triumph to all efforts, great and small.

Sometimes I can hardly believe that the shy little boy who used to hide himself and his dreams behind his camera is now using the camera to show millions of people how to bring their own dreams to light. My childhood dream of being a professional photographer has come true, and it has given birth to new dreams. It has given birth to *Sepia Dreams.*

—*matthew jordan smith*
New York City
November 2001

introduction

by Vanessa Williams

Everyone dreams. And, of course, everyone doubts. Often alone and sometimes afraid, we curl up under the covers of our lives. There we build elaborate fantasies, dreams of the future that, too often, fade into the past as we awaken to the dawn of our daily realities. In *Sepia Dreams,* my friend Matthew Jordan Smith takes your dreams and places them in the palm of your hand.

When Matthew first told me he was compiling this book of words and images from African-American achievers, I was thrilled. I couldn't wait! The first thing I wanted to do was run out and buy copies for myself, my kids, and all of my friends. Now that I have seen the realization of all the years of hard work that Matthew has devoted to this project, I am even more excited and unbelievably proud to have been included in this powerful guide to making *your* dreams come true.

I wish that I had had a book like this at the beginning of my career to lead me and my high hopes through the mysterious maze in which we all become lost, at one time or another, when our dreams collide with our realities. Now those of us who are just beginning, those of us who are trying to keep on keeping on—and even those of us who feel like giving up—have a new vision. We have *Sepia Dreams.*

Sepia Dreams is a unique collection of fifty photographs and motivational interviews with African-American celebrities who speak candidly about the drive, determination, and spiritual vision that made them successful. It combines beautiful images and inspiring words with practical advice about the actions and the attitude necessary to succeed at any endeavor.

In their own words, our most beloved artists, athletes, and entertainers tell us hilarious and moving stories of how they became successful and—just as important—how they deal with the responsibilities and rewards of their success. They also provide insightful and uplifting advice for anyone who has ever had a dream worth living and is searching for useful information about how to make that dream come true.

Majestic and captivating photographs of each celebrity accompany each success story, helping to bring its message and meaning to life. These images are more than mere documentation. They are a celebration of African-American beauty and stature that are sure to inspire African-American readers, whose deep longing for such images is widely recognized. As I learned when I became the first Black Miss America, and as I am reminded by those who have supported me throughout my career, for African-Americans, images of Black beauty are much more than pretty pictures. In a culture that often values looks above health and happiness, they serve to inspire as well as to build confidence and pride. Most of all, they restore the self-esteem of so many that have been damaged by countless depictions of Black people as unattractive.

Even before they read a single word, readers will be enchanted and motivated by the images of beauty, grace, and dignity that *Sepia Dreams* shows them. By depicting African-American success through pictures as well as words, *Sepia Dreams* provides immediate inspiration as well as long-term motivation.

The first time I had the opportunity to shoot with Matthew, I was living out one of my own biggest dreams—starring on Broadway in *Kiss of the Spiderwoman.* Although I have starred in numerous films and television shows, becoming a Broadway star had always been my oldest and dearest childhood dream, one that during the most difficult days of my career seemed hopelessly out of reach. Through perseverance, hard work, and the support of family, friends, fans, and faith, I finally turned my dream of singing and dancing on a Broadway stage into a reality.

And Matthew Jordan Smith was there to beautifully capture that moment so that I would never forget what I had achieved and how far I had come. Through the years, Matthew has documented my life through countless professional and personal transitions, and he always seems to make me smile. He has seen me at my most vulnerable—and at my most pregnant—moments. For nearly a decade of magazine covers, makeup ads, and movie posters, I have trusted Matthew Jordan Smith with one of my most prized possessions—my image.

Over the years we have become good friends. Matthew has become one of my favorite "Imagicians," and he has described me as one of his favorite muses. Matthew's extraordinary gift as a photographer is the reason why so many people, whose work depends on how we are represented, turn to him when we want to look our most beautiful and powerful.

As any African-American entertainer will tell you, our challenges in the entertainment industry go far beyond breaking through barriers and shattering glass ceilings. We must always be concerned not only with how we can cross boundaries and achieve success but how we will be represented once we succeed. It is a difficult—and sometimes painful—struggle for us to find people who truly know how to make Black faces and bodies look their best without denying or hiding who we are. This challenge is not based on vanity but on necessity and personal dignity. Not only do we work in an industry where "image is everything" but many of us are committed to providing our children and our communities with images that will help make them proud and powerful.

We turn to Matthew because he does more than just make us look good. He celebrates who we are—personally and culturally. He combines his technical skill with his creative vision to prove beyond a shadow of a doubt that "Black is beautiful" is more than a slogan—it is a visual and spiritual reality. His photographs capture more than our looks; they hold up a mirror to our inner lives, our characters, our personalities, even our dreams.

By presenting our photographs together with our words, he has united the truth of our beauty with the truth of our being. The result is an amazing testament to African-American beauty, passion, and power. A book like this one is long overdue. For those of us who are afraid that pursuing our goals means selling out, *Sepia Dreams* shows us how to achieve success on our own terms. It tells us how to live our dreams without losing our dignity.

At the same time, *Sepia Dreams* will empower everyone, of any background, who has ever had a dream. Matthew Jordan Smith has gathered together an extraordinary group of inspiring people and allowed them to share their dreams, fears, and hopes for the future. The contributors to *Sepia Dreams* provide priceless information for everyone about how to get to the top and stay there, without surrendering yourself and your dream along the way. Even those of us who have made many of our dreams come true will find in *Sepia Dreams* valuable lessons about how to stay true to our paths, how to keep growing beyond our wildest dreams, and how to take others with us into a future that we can all create together. *Sepia Dreams* has given me incredible insights from people whom I, as an artist and businesswoman, have admired for years. The contributors to *Sepia Dreams* give readers the advice and support that so many of us long for. Reading *Sepia Dreams* is like sitting in a room full of incredible, ideal mentors who hold your hand and spark your imagination as they impart their hard-earned lessons of a lifetime—lessons of caution, lessons of wisdom, lessons of inspiration.

So no matter who you are and no matter what you do, sit back and savor the unique stories and uncommon strengths that *Sepia Dreams* has to offer. Let the extraordinary individuals whose voices and visions live on these pages share their images and their insights with you. *Sepia Dreams* is guaranteed to help you turn your dreams into your destiny.

sepia dreams

karl kani

ambition

*The minute you think that you've made it, you don't have anything to
strive for anymore. Make something happen. Don't sit around—
the world ain't gonna come to you, you've got to go to the world.*

i had one particular goal when I started out—to dress the world and to dress
my people so that we don't have to depend on other designers to tell us what
fashion is all about. So that we don't have to depend on other people to take our
creativity from the streets, to exploit it, to make it seem like they created it. I
wanted to help us stay in control of our images and of our resources.

The main key to staying on top is never to lose that driving force you had when
you started. If you lose that, there's always somebody hungrier than you are out
there trying to get to where you are. Every day when you wake up, act as if you
don't have anything because the minute you think that you've made it, you don't
have anything to strive for anymore. That's my whole philosophy. Get up, go out
there, and *do* something. Make something happen. Don't sit around—the world
ain't gonna come to you, you've got to go to the world.

When I came out with my jeans, I realized I had to have a name for them. I decided to name them after myself, but "Karl Williams Jeans" didn't really have a
nice ring to it. "Can I?" has always been *my* question: Can I really achieve success
in the garment industry? Can I make this happen? So I just kind of put Karl and "Can
I" together as Karl Kani, and every day I have to answer that question—yes, I can.
It's like a reminder to myself to keep striving for the best all the time. No doubt.

I was born in Costa Rica, but I grew up in Brooklyn, New York. My parents had
a great work ethic. They showed me that you had to go out there and work. They

taught me that nothing comes easy. When I was twelve, I had a paper route and then I got a job delivering circulars to office buildings. That was my method of getting money—I worked for it. You know why I did all of those jobs? Because I wanted clothes. Growing up in the projects, there was a lot of peer pressure to dress well and to have the best clothes. That's what got me into fashion. I liked clothes, but I wanted to be different from everybody else.

My father used to get his clothes tailor-made. I used to watch him buy the fabric, go to his tailor, and have him make some pants. One time I asked him if I could design my own outfit, and he let me. After I designed my first outfit, everybody in the project was saying, "Yo, that's cool. Where did you get that?" That's what made me see that I could make something that people wanted. I started making clothes for other people as a hobby, but eventually I realized it could really become a business. The idea of mixing music and fashion hit me when hip-hop music was becoming popular in the early 80s. We were shopping a lot, coming up with a lot of styles, but African-Americans weren't getting anything in return for contributing to and supporting the garment industry. We were never featured in ads or catalogues. I thought, *I can't really rap or dance so at least let me dress these people and be part of this culture.* Even then, I knew that hip-hop was going to be around for a very long time.

I left home when I was nineteen. I was on a mission to become a successful entrepreneur. I went to California, learned about the garment industry, and started my own company. My first big break was when I hooked up with Dr. Dre, and they started wearing my clothes on *Yo! MTV Raps.* I also partnered with Cross Colours, one of the biggest Black-owned garment companies at the time. I learned so much from them, but in 1994, I split off so that I could do my own thing. At first it was very difficult for me to get into the major stores because they didn't know where to place my clothes. But we kept banging on doors and kids kept asking for our product. We created a space for ourselves in the stores and in the culture. Today, it's a lot easier for Black designers to get into the business because we paved the way for people to do their thing, which is great.

More young African-Americans need to develop entrepreneurial skills. There are so many opportunities for us today because of the Internet and the popularity of street culture. The streets are really ruling the world. Street culture and the street market are a powerful driving force internationally. Young Black people are recognized throughout the world as having something unique and important to contribute, and we've got to take advantage of that. Look at your community, look at your own situation, and see where the voids are, find a way to fill them. See what the people need and go out there and provide it for them.

It's good to know that you are going to face serious obstacles. To me, business is like warfare, and you've got to be prepared for war. Business isn't nice. That's why a lot of times people don't like people in business, because you've got to make difficult decisions that affect people's livelihoods and the way they live. You've got to associate yourself with good people and surround yourself with people who know how to do things *you* don't know how to do. You've got to be a visionary.

Everything that happened to me kind of happened just in time. Nothing happened too quickly. I see what happens to companies that grow too quickly—they don't usually last. It's good to take your time and do things right. God has definitely blessed my work. He's made me learn to practice patience. That's very hard, especially when you want to achieve so much and do really big things. But I've learned to take a backseat and let other people shine. I know my time is going to come around. When you're hot, you're hot, and when it's your time, it's your time. You've just got to stay in the game, and just keep doing things right. We also have to be able to just chill, to treat success as a norm for Black people.

It means a lot to me that people go out there, spend their money, and wear my name. So I definitely want to stand for something, and I want my name to stand for something. We want to go down in history for showing people that you can start from the streets and become anything that you want to become as long as you are true to your vision. That's what I did—I saw where I wanted to go and I go there by being all about my dream. That's basically what Kani is all about, asking myself that question, "Can I?" And living the answer every day: "Yes!"

susan l. taylor

balance

When your emotional life is in balance, everything else works.
I see myself as a student of my own life. I'm always reaching for
something more.

the best advice that I ever got was to manage my personal life. That's something that I really took to heart and have focused on very carefully. All too often, people are successful in their professional world but in their personal world, things are chaotic and falling apart, and that affects every aspect of their lives. When you manage your personal world— when your emotional life is in balance—everything else works. That's why you need to get rid of all the "negaholics" in your life and surround yourself with nurturing friends and family.

You especially have to be clear about yourself, your life, and your aspirations. You need to clarify your intentions. I have always been very goal-oriented. Without goals I feel like a ship without a rudder. The challenge is to set our goals very carefully, to figure out a process for realizing them, and to break that process down into manageable daily tasks. When I do that, the books get written. And when I don't, the projects never get off the shelf.

In order to identify and achieve your goals, you must always keep in mind who you are and what creates happiness in your life. Spend quiet time getting to know yourself so you're not wanting to be someone else because you have *no* idea what another person's experience is. All too often people strive for things without knowing the kind of lifestyle they're going to live once they achieve them. Know whether or not you

want to travel. Know whether you want to be home with your family by six o'clock. Know what's important to you. Create your professional focus around those things that really make you happy and create the kind of inner support and sustenance that you need.

I never felt limited in terms of my possibilities because I've had people in my life who believed in me, even when I doubted myself. I was always inspired by my father and grandmother, who were both business people. My father had a ladies' boutique and worked in that store six days a week until, as my mother would say, "the last pair of stockings were sold." He taught me about tenacity, courage, and just burning the midnight oil.

Because of my family, I always saw myself as an entrepreneur. I wanted to do something that I would be great at so I created a cosmetics company in 1970 called Nequai, after my daughter. I didn't know anyone who owned a cosmetics company, but I saw a need. I knew that I couldn't find makeup shades that were right for me, and at the time, very few companies were creating products for women of color. The *Essence* editors heard about me, brought me to *Essence,* and that's how I got where I am today.

I was probably a lot more confident at twenty-three than I am at fifty-three. Because here I was at twenty-three years old without any academic, literary, or journalistic credentials, but I made my way to *Essence* and interviewed for a job as a beauty editor believing that I could do it. When I got the opportunity, I didn't have the skill. I had the eye, but I didn't have the skill.

Later, when *Essence* offered me the editor-in-chief position, at first I turned it down because I hadn't gone to college; I didn't have a literary background. I said I was a cosmetologist, not a journalist, and didn't feel that I really had the "goods" to do the job. That's why it's so important to surround yourself with people who nourish you and who believe in you. I went home and called a good friend and he said to me, "You have exactly what our people need, specifically what Black women need. You can do it." And that's all I needed to hear. That gave me the courage to step into Ed Lewis's office the next day and put my hand on either side of his desk and say, "I'm ready."

The "In the Spirit" column in *Essence* is sort of my public diary. I probably write it as much for myself as for our readers. That's one of the reasons I continue to write the column although I left the editor-in-chief position to pursue new goals in the company. I'm writing about what I need to know and what I'm trying to live. I know what nourishes me from within, and when I move away from those things, my life really spins out of control. I find that a lack of confidence, a little depression, some self-doubt—all of those things—begin to rear their heads. But the moment that I begin doing what I *need* to do everyday, which means putting on my spiritual armor, my life works. Putting on my spiritual armor means getting up every morning and giving myself to *myself* before I give myself away. It means thinking quietly for a moment and really just giving thanks for the day, thinking about all the blessings in my life. It also means thinking about what I'm going to do for the day and taking anything off the agenda that's going to make me rush and be crazy, simplifying the day because it's always so crowded.

I think quiet time is the most important time that any of us can take, and what is gravely missing in all of our lives. We all need quiet, reflective time in which there is no music, no distraction, no one's voice except that inner voice, that still, soft voice of God. Quiet time allows us to hear that voice within us and empowers us to be present so that we can hear the wisdom as it pours forth.

i believe that all adults, whether they're famous or not, have a responsibility to influence younger people positively. I think that all adults have to be careful about what we do because we set an example that our children, whether they're our biological children or not, will follow.

I think we can accept our responsibility to young people by committing our personal resources to them. By that I mean showing up in their lives, being present. Each of us has his or her hand on a young person's shoulder. We can help them by listening, really listening, to what they're saying to us, by asking questions about what they're thinking and feeling, and by using our collective power to ensure that poor children have access to the things that middle-class children take for granted.

The pain that I have in my heart is that we're not doing all that we can do in the wealthiest country in the world and as the most affluent and greatly blessed Black people anywhere on this planet. We're not doing enough for our poor sisters and brothers who are struggling.

I emphasize the combination of spirituality and enterpreneurship because I believe that together they will form a foundation of love and security for our people and give us the wings that we need to fly.

I am a person who is really on a path. I am really trying to look deeply within myself, and I am consciously and passionately trying to be the best person that I can be so that I can do some good in the world. I'm still striving to get to another plateau. So I really do see myself as a student. Always learning, growing, unfolding. I love my life. I think it is getting better and better and the best is yet to come for me and for our people. That's what I always feel. I believe the best is yet to come.

lela rochon

beauty

*One of the most important things that I've learned in my career is that
pretty doesn't last forever. It will fade. I knew I had to go deeper.*

the greatest misconception about being an actress is that it's easy. That it's
easy, and that everybody can do it. Many people can do it, but it takes a lot of
work. The main thing that I hope people realize about me is that my success didn't
fall in my lap. I've worked very, very, *very* hard, and I love what I do. I know that
you get a foot in the door a lot of times just on looks. But once I got through the
door, what I did in the room was always up to me and my talent as an actress. Although I think that beauty is, in many ways, eternal, one of the most important
things that I've learned in my career is that pretty doesn't last forever. It will fade.
And then what will you have as an instrument? What will your instrument be?
Even when you are at your most attractive as an actress, you just can't be cute and
jump up and do it. I knew that I had to really study and work at it. I knew I had to
go deeper.

You can't act if you have no life experiences, especially difficult ones. You have
to have something to draw from. Life is what gives you character. It makes you
stronger. For example, twenty-nine was a really hard age for me. I wasn't working.
I had no success at dating. I'd already had enough success and fame so that people wanted to date me because of who I was—or of what sexual fantasies they
had of me—but nobody wanted to get to know *me,* and my heart, and who I am.
Every time I have to do a scene, I can draw on my pain and get to that emotional
place that is the source of my best work.

As an actress, I'm always intrigued by the mystery of the future, by the unknown. I've always had goals, but things never happened my way. They happened in the way that God wanted them to happen, and I've learned to accept that and look forward to it.

I have been blessed with two wonderful parents who have been married for over thirty-five years. Had I not had the upbringing, the morals, and the values that my parents placed within me, I would be lost in Hollywood. The support of my parents has had a tremendous impact on my success. When I changed my mind every week as a child—"Mommy, I want to be a lawyer. Mommy, I want to be a doctor. Mommy, I want to be a journalist"—they always said, "That's great, baby. Whatever you want to do." If I had wanted to be President of the United States, they would have supported me. At the same time, they also helped me focus on working hard at things that were important to me. At one point, I was involved in a lot of different school activities, and my mother said, "You're good at everything, but you need to excel at something." That stuck with me. That's one of the reasons I never really gave up on acting.

As a little girl I never dreamed about being an actress, but when I was in college at Cal State–Dominguez Hills, I met Marla Gibbs, whom people will remember was the housekeeper on *The Jeffersons*. She used to have a school called Crossroads, for Los Angeles children who didn't have exposure to theater. I did a play there one summer and I got bit by the acting bug.

I also danced for fun during college, and when I was seventeen, I had people approach me about doing a couple of music videos. I did one for Lionel Richie and one for Luther Vandross. After that, I met with a commercial agent and they signed me. I thought of it in terms of my education. I said, "Oh, this is good. I can get money for school, for books." Then I booked the first couple of auditions I attended. I didn't know how rare that was. I eventually got a TV movie and other jobs, but there was only so much I could do, because it was really important to me to finish college.

A year before graduating from Cal State University, I auditioned and got a commercial that ended up running for a long time. As a result, I got a role on *The Cosby Show*. I played Lisa Bonet's best friend, a troubled teenager who got pregnant. That particular episode was nominated for an Emmy for that season so it got a lot of attention. From that, I started getting even more auditions.

That's when I started to study acting seriously. I got my degree in journalism because that was another serious interest. If I weren't an actress, I would probably be doing the news. And still, I minored in theater and sociology because I realized that if I was seriously going to pursue acting it wasn't going to be easy. I spent all my money on acting classes in Hollywood. Classes taught me how to work with other actors, which is extremely important. I think my career started to turn, though, when I stopped taking group classes and started working with a private coach. Classes are great, but in many cases, you just want to land a job, so I think you need a coach.

I would say that my first big break was *Harlem Nights*. My performance attracted a great deal of attention, but there were no movies after that. After *Harlem Nights*, I was offered a soap opera, which I chose not to do. I wanted to do movies, but there were no movies for Black actresses. My next movie wasn't until two years later. It was another Eddie Murphy movie—*Boomerang*.

At that time, everybody was on this *Boyz N the Hood* craze, but they thought I was a little bit too sophisticated to be the girl in the hood, although that's where I grew up. I have a very accurate sense of what it means to be "from the hood," but Hollywood stereotypes put everybody from "the hood" into a small box, and I didn't fit into it even though that was my actual background. They don't really have a lot of imagination. Even when there were parts they thought were right for me, I would always lose out to the same actresses. They have their favorite Black girls, and that's it.

I wanted to quit right before I got *Waiting to Exhale.* I just felt that guest-starring on sitcoms—coming in and saying, "Baby, are you okay?"—was not what I wanted to do. I told myself that if this is what it's about, I'll give it one more year and then I'm going to do something else. I let it go. And that's when it happened for me.

since then, I have worked very hard to get to that higher level. Success is about competition, about rising to the level of the competition that sets the standards for your profession. The more you work and stay active, the better you become. But when it really counts, you also have to focus on specific goals. If you are a woman who wants to become an actress, you need to start young, and you have to really, really want it because it's going to be painful. It's going to hurt, but I think the rewards are like no other profession's.

I know that success in this business is fleeting, but I want to act until I'm a very old lady. I love it. I love that high you get when you really nail a scene. I just hope that I make my mark and do my share of what I'm here to do with my time on this earth. I see myself as a good person, a kind person, a good wife, and a very talented woman who has only just begun.

smokey robinson

blessings

I have no complaints about my life. It's a blessing. I have been through some real crises, but so what? I've had many peaks and valleys in my life, and the valleys have always made me appreciate the peaks.

i am living a life that I absolutely love. If, on the day before I was born, the Lord had come to me and said, "Hey, I want you to fill out this questionnaire as to what you want your life to be," I would have filled out what I'm living right now! I am living my dream. I can't beat that. I never dared to believe that this would actually be my life. I wanted it to be so bad, but I just wouldn't let myself get my hopes up. So when it happened, I felt so blessed. Not everybody gets a chance to do what I've done. And I always look at it like that. I have no complaints about my life. It's a blessing. I have been through some real crises, but so what? I've had many peaks and valleys in my life, and the valleys have always made me appreciate the peaks.

I think that writing was the Lord's calling for me because I've been writing songs ever since I can remember. I wrote my first song when I was about six. I'll never forget this because I was in the first grade. We were having a school play at Dwyer Elementary School in Detroit. At the beginning of the program, my teacher had written this melody at the piano. I asked her if I could write some words for it. She agreed so that's what I did, and I sang it in the play. That was the first time I ever wrote a song. I've been writing ever since.

When I was younger, I thought I might be an electrical engineer or that I would be a baseball player because I was pretty good, but singing, which was my first dream, just seemed too far-fetched to me, man. It just seemed too far away. Too

impossible. Then one day I went to see Frankie Lymon and the Teenagers at the Broadway Capital Theater. All of a sudden the dream didn't seem that far. I said, "Well, golly, if these guys can do it, maybe I can do it!" But I still wasn't sure.

I grew up in one of those Detroit neighborhoods where a lot of people became famous in show business, like Diana Ross and Aretha Franklin. I lived near the Four Tops. I've known the Temptations since high school. We used to have song battles where all the groups would get together and compete. I believe that in every town, in every city, in the whole world, there is a bunch of talented young people. It's just that they have no outlets. But in Detroit, we had Berry Gordy. He was a young Black man who had a dream, and he had the instinct and inner ability to pull it off. It took a lot of doing.

I was singing with a group called the Miracles, and I was in college studying electrical engineering when I met Berry in August of 1957. He was writing these hit songs for Jackie Wilson at the time, and Jackie Wilson was my number-one singing idol. I was sixteen or seventeen when we auditioned for Jackie Wilson's managers. They told us, "Hey, there's already the Platters, and you've got a guy singing high and a girl in the group, and you'll never make it because you've got to change your format and blah, blah, blah." The whole time there was this young guy sitting over in the corner. I thought he was waiting to audition next because he looked like he was about seventeen, nineteen at the most. When we walked out after they had rejected us, we were very dejected. This guy came out and said, "Hey, man, where'd you get those songs you sang?" I told him, "Well, I wrote them." He said, "Yeah? A couple of them I liked." I'm thinking to myself that he wants to sing a couple of them for his audition. Then he said, "I'm Berry Gordy." I said, "Berry Gordy who writes the songs for Jackie Wilson?" My mouth dropped open. I could not believe that this cat right here was Berry Gordy. I had always loved his songwriting. So I said, "Oh, man!" He said, "Got any more songs?" I had a loose-leaf notebook, man, filled with about one hundred songs. I sang about twenty songs for Berry that day. Even though we went to that audition and got rejected, I guess it was my fate. The Lord had planned this for me because Berry Gordy just happened to be there. I hooked up with him, and about a year or so after that, we started Motown. It was meant to be.

I've learned that you are first and foremost a human being. You get into this, and it's a lifestyle. But I think we all make the world go around. People see being a garbageman as one of the lowliest jobs. But what if there was no guy who wanted to pick up the garbage? The world would be in trouble. I think the world could certainly do without a bunch of people in show business more so than it could do without a bunch of guys who pick up the garbage. So how can a person in show business think that they're so high and mighty and think that the garbageman or a cab driver or a grocer or the butcher is below them? If it weren't for those people having your records and supporting your work, then what you are doing wouldn't matter anyway. I know that for a fact. In show business, you are what the public *allows* you to be. If it weren't for them, you wouldn't be whoever it is you think you are. You can never forget that. This is my job. I hope I can do it well, and I hope that when I go somewhere and perform I can make somebody happy.

The love of writing itself is what inspires me to do it. I know that it's a gift, and that's how I look at it because very seldom does a day ever go by that a part of a song doesn't come to me—a melody or a phrase or some words. I don't really need some sort of special inspiration to do it. I don't have to be sad to write a sad song or happy to write a happy song. I don't have to take some time off and go to the mountains so I can write. No. I can write on the toilet. On the bus. In the plane. Wherever it hits me. I'm blessed. It's a gift. If you are going to be a songwriter, make sure that your songs have continuity, structure, and meaning. Make sure they tell a story. You have also got to be a strong person. You have to be a person who can tolerate setbacks. Because that's what show business is. It is very fickle. Show business is "Okay, you're riding high today, but you're down tomorrow." You have to be somebody who can tolerate being slapped down and then get back up and keep on steppin'.

Love is the neverending subject. Love is forever, I hope. I hope that as long as there are two people on the Earth, in the world, that there will be love. Now I have written a couple of songs about political things and dances. Never about a car that I can remember, but people do write songs about cars—the '57 Chevy and the "this" and the "that." But all of those things become passé, you see. The political situation of that day is passé tomorrow. The car of that day is passé tomorrow. The dance of that day is passé tomorrow. But love is never passé. Love is constantly here. Constantly turning itself over. Constantly becoming a different thing to the same person. When I write a song, I want it to be a song that would have been significant if I had written it a hundred years earlier or that will be significant a hundred years from the day that I write it. So, I write about love. I love love.

The most important thing in my life is being happy and making those around me happy. It's important for me to be positive. I work hard to focus on the best things about my life. I don't dwell on what has gone wrong in the past or what is going wrong at the time. I always remember that I'm very, very, very blessed. I try to take care of myself because I want to do what I'm doing for the rest of my life. I love my life. I'm going to live it to the fullest.

tyson beckford

community

*I always remember that I'm representing everybody so I try to make
sure that when I do things, I do big things. Big things make big
differences.*

when I started out, I had nothing to lose and a whole lot to gain. Whenever I get
low on energy, I always say, "Remember how things were before. You don't ever
want to go back to the way things were." I always remember that I'm representing everybody so I try to make sure that when I do things, I do *big* things. Big
things make big differences in the game.

I grew up in The Bronx in a pretty rough neighborhood. I had four brothers, but
I was closest to my one brother, Patrick. He had the most influence on me as I was
growing up. When you see your older brother, you want to look like him, dress like
him, act like him. You want to go out and do the same things that he does. I got in
trouble numerous times when I was a kid, but because I was so young, I just
laughed it off. I told myself, "Man, that ain't nothing."

I think what saved me was losing my brother to the streets when I was twenty-
one. It definitely let me know that street life is for real. My brother would have
been a phenomenal actor. He was in the theater, and he was really good at it. But
the streets just consumed him.

When I was first told that I should pursue modeling, I was a knucklehead. People used to tell me to look into it, and I'd say, "Yeah, yeah, whatever." But I started
taking it seriously one day when some people from *The Source,* a hip-hop magazine, approached me. I had just gotten locked up. It was only for one night, but I
hated being in that cell. When I got out, I was asking myself, "Wow, brother,
what's wrong with you?"

Right after that my uncle, cousin, and I were sitting in Washington Square Park in Greenwich Village. It was a summer day, and this guy and this girl came up to me and said, "Yo, you've really got interesting eyes. Have you ever thought about modeling?" I was being that hard-core New Yorker, saying, "Naw. I'm not interested. Beat it. Leave me alone." Finally they said, "What have you got to lose?" So I tried it.

I started by doing that one shoot, and I got some freelance work. At first I was, like, "Everybody in America's looking at this? Wow, this is cool." Then I wasn't making any money so I went back to the streets and started messing around with the hustling game again. All I can remember was my brother, Patrick, saying to me, "Yo, that's not smooth. You've got this talent. You need to go on with it." When my brother told me that, I said, "You know what? You're right." That's when I seriously got into it. I was really chasing it. I started building a little name for myself, and I said, "All right, I'm ready to take it to the next level."

When Patrick died, it hit me really hard. I completely gave up hope and withdrew from everything and everyone for a while. Then I remembered what he'd been trying to tell me, and I knew what he would have wanted me to do, so, eventually, I started to reach out to the world again. One day, I met the actor Kadeem Hardison, who told me his mother was this incredible modeling agent named Bethann Hardison, so I went to see her. When I walked into her office, I was probably looking more like a thug than a model, but she gave me a chance. Once I signed with her, she really helped me make things happen.

In the beginning there was no market, and there were days that I just wanted to quit. Bethann would give me pep talks and tell me, "Look. You've got Europe under your belt. Everyone in Europe loves you, and you just want to quit?" I would say, "Well, Bethann, there's a lot of pressure. I'm going to these photo shoots and casting calls, and there are forty white guys and little old me and maybe another brother whose agency kind of forced him to come." So you would have two Black brothers who didn't really want to be there because we didn't have a chance.

But that changed. When I went to different castings, I started seeing more and more brothers coming in for these gigs. When I told my friends about it, I started opening the minds of everybody in my neighborhood. At the same time, my ads started opening the minds of everybody in the industry. The whole game just switched and it's funny now how I go to a casting call or a fashion show, and all the white boys will turn and look. Now they're the ones who are, like, "Oh!"

The game definitely did change, and a lot of people give me credit for that, but I didn't do it by myself. It was done by my Black community. Hip-hop music and the whole era of urban appeal have had a big impact on the industry and have given me a beautiful life. Everyone who went out and supported whatever I did has had an impact. It was, like, if I put something on, I was putting it on for a whole community—not just Black, not just White, not just Latino or Asian. It was as if I was doing it for everybody. I threw everything I had into every ad I shot. And to this day, I do the same thing.

If I could go back, I definitely would have hit the books harder and stayed out of trouble. Most of all, I wish that I had just been able to hold on to my brother and say, "This is not the move for us. Let's do something else." But I know that he's with me every day. Some nights and some days you don't want to go and do what you have to do. You have to look out for something else—for someone or something else that inspires you, and that keeps you going.

Now I have a son. His name is Jordan. Jordan is a powerful river and a powerful name. I'm so excited about seeing my son grow up, seeing what type of individual he'll grow up to be. I hope that he'll take everything that I'm trying to instill in him and that people will respect him for who he is. We need to lay down some serious groundwork for the next generation. We have to show them that it's not a White man's world, and it never really was. It's just that we were too ignorant to open our eyes and see what we could have been doing and should have been doing.

These days, people are so into getting the platinum chains, the fancy cars, the nice houses. What are you doing for your community? How are you uplifting your people? A lot of kids grow up, and they're so spoiled. They get everything they want. They have to know how to work for it. That's what I learned. Today, I see myself as a strong individual who is just busting his butt to get to the next level of success. I'm not there yet, but I'm on my way.

reggie miller

competitiveness

No matter how long you play—even if it's only two minutes—make it the best two minutes of your life. If it's the whole game, give it your best effort, but always be ready.

to me, basketball is a lot like chess. You're always acting and counteracting, anticipating your opponent's next move. The competition in basketball is mental as well as physical. You can rattle your opponent just by talking to him. When you've got him, the crowd gets into it, and you just feed off of that. I still get butterflies before a game because it's the unexpected. You never know what's going to happen. I think that's the best element of sports. You don't know the outcome. Ultimately, it's all about focusing—being mentally prepared to face any obstacle and any challenge. A lot of times it works, but sometimes, as much as you focus, it might not be there. But it's all about repetition, doing the same thing over and over until you get it right.

Always losing at basketball when I was a kid has helped me get where I am today. Not necessarily in basketball, but in life in general because you're always going to face obstacles. I learned to always work hard, to overcome whatever obstacles exist, and then to show 'em in the end.

I never set out to be a professional basketball player. I just knew that if I worked hard, something good would happen. I had a good base, a good family structure. My parents were strict but in a loving way. They supported us, but they never pushed us into sports. Today, I think a lot of parents push their kids into sports, trying to live their athletic dreams through their kids, but my parents never did that. My sister Cheryl and I wanted to hang around our older brothers so we just copied what they did and one of the things they did was to play basketball.

Cheryl has had the biggest influence on me as a player. We were closer than any two siblings could be. People don't understand how hard we pushed one another. She has been in the national spotlight since the age of thirteen. When you're growing up with a sister who is considered the best woman's basketball player ever, that challenges you. I always had someone there to push me. I was always getting beat on the playground by Cheryl, my brothers, and the other kids in the neighborhood. I think that really steeled me and upped my drive to work even harder.

When I was growing up, baseball was my first love. I was a much, much better baseball player than I was a basketball player. But in basketball, you feel the excitement, the crowd is into it, everything is so electric. I need to have that adrenaline rush so I decided that I was going to concentrate on basketball and sell my cleats.

I was always a late bloomer. I'm 6'7" now, but when I entered high school I was only 5'9". I was shorter than everyone else. The coach would never let me start because there was a guy, Dave Myers, who was ahead of me on the team. The coach loved him, the community loved him, the school loved him. One time, we were at an away game, but he only had his home uniform, which he was not allowed to wear, so the coach says, "Reggie, I guess you're starting." I had never played in a game so my whole goal was to score 10 points. I had never even done that. So the coach started me, and I went out and scored 32 points. The next game, I scored 40 points. The third game I scored 42 points. That's when I got my confidence, that's where everything started.

But I often look back and think what if Dave Myers hadn't forgotten his jersey? Would I ever have been given an opportunity? I probably never would have played. I probably would have been his backup the whole time. So things happen for a reason. I always tell kids that no matter how long you play—even if it's only two minutes—make it the best two minutes of your life. If it's the whole game, give it your best effort, but always be ready.

I always knew I could outwork the competition. That was my whole goal. In high school, after basketball practice, I'd come home and shoot for another couple of hours. I always said, "Anytime I'm wide open, I want to make every single shot." So I would shoot three, four, five hundred times at the same spot, over and over and over again until I'd make ten, fifteen, twenty in a row. I got into that mindset. I was always shooting and shooting and shooting.

I still practice whenever I can. There is a misconception that once you turn pro, you don't have to go to practices anymore. That's why a lot of these young players don't get better. You tend to work toward your strengths, and you try to ignore your weaknesses. But in today's age of videotape and scouting, you're forced to work on your weaknesses. That's why I always tell kids, if you're right-handed and can't dribble with your left, comb your hair with your left hand, eat with your left, tie your shoes with your left hand, do something all day with your left hand. Get your "off" hand as strong as your best hand.

The summer is the time to improve your game. During the season, you don't have time to work as hard as you want to, but you have all the time in the world during the summer. A lot of people don't understand that. Magic Johnson, Byron Scott, Michael Cooper, those guys really taught me that when I was at UCLA. I learned so much from playing every day with them and understanding the work ethic that goes into the game.

In my whole life, the thing that I'm most proud of is that I graduated from UCLA. I wish they'd put a moratorium on the kids coming into the NBA out of high school. I think they ought to make it a rule that you've just got to go to college for at least two years. I don't blame the kids because the money is shoved in their faces, but they just come in with nothing but raw talent. All they see on TV is Michael Jordan and Allen Iverson, but they don't see the work that goes into achieving that level of excellence. They just think they're going to come in and do what they see on TV. They don't make time for the basics. That's what they teach you in college and a lot more.

In the NBA, your role models become your competitors so you want to play the game the right way and have the same dedication that they have. When I was coming up, I tried to compete with all the stars because, in the age of CNN and SportsCenter, if you can dog them out you're going to see it on television. I tried to make my name off of Michael Jordan because if you make a name off of Michael, it spreads. I love going against the younger kids because now they're coming after me. That, in itself, is a challenge. I like to teach the kids a lesson.

The best way to influence the next generation of athletes is through education and talking with them about the sport. They need to realize that you never want to set your goals so high that you can't attain them but you do want them up there. Then, you have to work hard to achieve them.

If I could start over, I wouldn't do anything differently because I grew up with a wonderful family, and I've worked hard for everything I have achieved. The best advice anyone ever gave me was not to take anything for granted. The best advice I could give to a young person who wanted to become an athlete is just to believe in yourself. Believe in yourself, don't doubt yourself, and even when you're down, play till the horn sounds off.

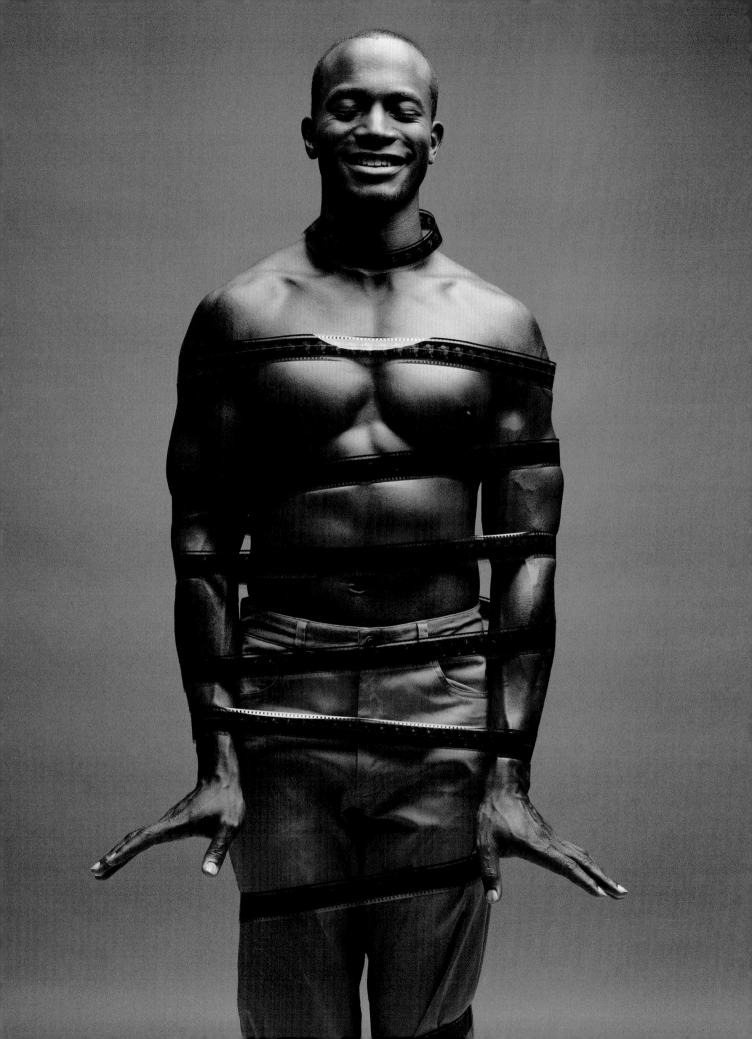

taye diggs

confidence

*The arts are where I found my confidence. I found who I was as a
person. It was a means of expression that came naturally. And it
was just plain fun.*

first of all, I always knew that I was going to make it. Deep down. I don't know
if it was because of a higher power or the confidence my mom and pops instilled
in me. I do know that I never took rejection as badly as everybody else did. I would
get hyped on something, and if I didn't get it, I'd be disappointed. But I always
tried to focus on other aspects of my life.

I focused on what brought me enjoyment—I choreographed, I was always in
dance class, always playing soccer in the park, things like that. I was always trying
to do other things so that if one thing didn't give me happiness for that day, I could
go and do something else and be fulfilled. I still try to keep that up. It's a major part
of how I do things.

The reason I act is because, as a kid, I just loved to pretend. Today, I truly enjoy
the connection of acting whether it's on stage or on film or on TV, or even for a
commercial. There's electricity that happens when two people connect through
acting—when you get on the same wavelength as someone else—just from pretending. I feel like I'm back when I was a kid, playing superheroes or cowboys and
Indians. Most importantly, the arts are where I found my confidence. I found who
I was as a person. It was a means of expression that came naturally. And it was
just plain fun.

More than anything else, my mother's love of the theater influenced my acting.
She was always there, very gently pushing me. She encouraged me to do a play

in seventh grade, and from that point on, I was sold. She convinced me to go to a performing arts high school where I tried everything—dance, voice, acting, tennis, soccer. It was a busy time.

I was considered a nerd in high school. I enjoyed sports but I was always too small and too skinny and not strong enough so I couldn't hang out with the popular clique. At that time, I really loved *A Soldier's Story* with Denzel Washington because I wore glasses and I was dark-skinned. Back in the day, dark skin wasn't in. But when I saw Denzel—he was dark, and he wore glasses, and he was debonair and handsome and strong—he made me think, *I can be like that. I want to be like that.* So I took my little bit of money and bought myself some used round gold frames so I could have his style. Denzel had a serious effect on me.

After high school, I decided to go to Syracuse University and major in voice. I thought I would be an opera singer, but that wasn't as much fun as I thought it would be so I decided to study musical theater. When I was a senior, my program had a showcase production for New York agents, and that's how I found an agent. After graduation, I moved to New York.

I had done summer stock in college, and I worked at Busch Gardens theme park, but my first substantial job with dignity was the musical *Carousel.* After that, I worked for Disney in Japan. I did a Caribbean Cabaret over there from which I have tapes that are very entertaining, to say the least. From there I was cast in the musical *Rent,* and my first major film role was in *How Stella Got Her Groove Back.*

I don't think I would do anything differently in my professional life, but I do wish that I had put more emphasis on my education. Although I completed college, I wish that I had paid more attention to academics as well as to the arts. I was so cocky. I was just so confident that things were going to work out for me in the arts that I was one of those kids who said, "Why am I going to need math? Why am I going to need science?" But as you get older, you value knowledge more, even if it's just for your own pride. You feel more equipped. It just feels good to know more.

I always tell aspiring actors to do whatever you need to do to make sure you're good. Take classes, practice, stay positive, be resilient, and stick with it. Leave yourself open. Don't have tunnel vision because, as an actor, you learn from everything. In school, there were all these kids who completely submerged themselves in theater, but I think that you need to become a whole person. You may be an actor, but you're not going to be playing an actor. You're going to be playing people in other walks of life—so play sports, go to parties, take other academic courses, do the things that make you a full person. Have a good head on your shoulders and a clear sense of what you want to do.

It's essential to keep everything in perspective. The most important thing to me now is family and friends. What's most fun about this whole Hollywood shtick is being able to enjoy it with other people.

I have no problem with being a role model. You have no choice *but* to be a role model when you're in the public eye. When people say "I'm not a role model," they're really saying that they don't *want* to be role models. But you have no choice. People are going to look up to you and someone, somewhere is going to want to be just like you in the same way that I wanted to be like Denzel Washington. That's the reality, and I'm up for it. I'm up for that responsibility. Although I would stress that what works for me might not necessarily work for you. But whatever I do, I will stand behind it. When I make mistakes, I'll stand up and admit it. I made a mistake, I'm human. But I know there's an opportunity to learn from my mistakes. Overall, being a role model goes hand in hand with how I would like to live—how I choose to live—anyway. Responsibly. With dignity. It's how I was raised. It's what would make my mother proud.

dominique dawes

determination

Someone could melt down my medals or steal them, and it wouldn't take away anything. For me success is not an object. It's not a destination—it's a journey.

i always remember why I'm doing things. I tell people always to make sure that the goals you set are for *you*, and to do it because you want to do it, because you love it and it makes you happy—not because it makes others happy. Don't let anyone else tell you what you should and shouldn't do. People have certain expectations of you, but you cannot let those expectations control your destiny. You need to focus on what *you* want, on what you want to do, and what you know you can do. My coach always told me, "It's you out there. Always remember that you're doing it for yourself, not for others."

When I was twelve, I came up with my own saying: D3—Determination, Dedication, Desire. I used to spray this saying with shaving cream on this huge mirror that I had in my bedroom. My parents hated it, but I used to spray it on—D3. I would just look at myself in the mirror, and it would bring positive vibes to me. It gave me strength and faith in myself. It's like a prayer. It's helped me get through tough times.

Sports help you discover yourself and develop yourself as a person. They help people realize things about themselves—their strengths and their weaknesses. But I don't think things should revolve around sports, because sports are not going to make or break the world. Medals and awards are not the most important thing. People could take the medals away, and I wouldn't miss them, because that's not what I remember. What I remember are the experiences that I have.

Someone could melt down my medals or steal them, and it wouldn't take away anything. For me success is not an object, it's not a destination—it's a journey.

I first began gymnastics at the age of six. Being an energetic child is what started it. I was the kind of child who runs around the house and breaks the furniture. My parents tried to channel my energy in a positive way. They thought, *Let's get this girl out of the house. Make her energy more useful.* And putting me into gymnastics definitely did that. I was a very dedicated gymnast. When I was six, I remember stepping into the gym and thinking, *Oh, I can do anything!,* and then being proved wrong immediately because I looked crazy compared to those other girls. But my coach saw potential in me. She kept me motivated, and she pushed me. She let me know that you have to sacrifice a lot, and train forty hours a week in the gym.

I started spending more time at the gym at about nine or ten, when I started competing. I would have to get up at 4:30 in the morning, wake my mom up, and have her bring me to the gym at 6 in the morning. We would train from 6 to 8, and my coach would take me to school. Then right after school, I'd come back for five more hours, 4 P.M. to 9 P.M., to train again. Just thinking about it now is, like, *Oh, my goodness!* That was just my life. You get used to it.

At the age of eleven everyone told me I was going to the Olympics, and I was telling them "No. That's not what I'm striving for now. I'm doing this sport because I love it." But at twelve, I finally decided that the Olympics were something that I did want to do. My coach and I set very intense schedules to work toward that. We made sure to focus on not just the physical aspect but on the mental aspect because a lot is about attitude. You may be a great, talented person but if your attitude stinks, you're not going to be as good as you should and could be.

So we worked on getting the whole package together, and I accomplished getting to my first Olympics when I was fifteen. When I was training for the second Olympics, for '96, I realized that I wanted to do a little bit more, I wanted to make a bigger impact, meaning that I wanted to be a leader. I wanted to stand out. I wanted to be the highest scorer on the team. And I was. I contributed on every single one of the events for the team competition so that I came away with an individual bronze medal and a team gold medal.

When I first started gymnastics, I was primarily known for my strength. People said I could tumble really well and that I was very strong, but I was not considered a flexible gymnast. But years and years of my coaches stretching me, of my sitting and watching TV while doing splits, of coming to the gym a little early or staying late, all of that really paid off. In 1996, I became known as one of the most flexible gymnasts on my Olympic team. Stretching became a ritual for me.

There were many times along the way that I wanted to quit. Sometimes I would have a horrible practice, and I'd be crying all the time, and I was like, "I'm no good." I had just won a gold medal for the USA and I'd still tell myself, "I'm not good enough, I shouldn't be doing this." Usually, it was pressure that I put on myself, but I didn't quit. You never want to be a quitter in life. You have to at least try—and that attitude is what pulled me through.

I always tell people that success comes from a team—Together Everyone Achieves More—that stands for TEAM. I'm not talking about just teammates on the basketball court, in the boardroom, or in the gymnastics arena. I'm talking about parents, teachers, and coaches—someone who's going to help you mentally as well as professionally. And also the Lord. For me to accomplish what I did as an individual, I had to have a team on my side. To succeed, you need positive people around. Don't hang with people who are going to bring you down, or criticize you, or speak badly about other people. Just surround yourself with loving people. Being an Olympian takes years of sacrifice from you, from your family, and from your coaches. It's not easy. It's a hard road but it's worth it in the end. Of course, I want to be remembered as an Olympic gymnast, but I also want to be remembered for the person that I am—as someone who was a very private person, but a star in her own way.

loretta devine

devotion

Anytime you devote yourself to something, you will eventually reap the benefits of it.

the most important thing with acting—or with anything—is to keep doing it. Don't give up. Have a lot of faith in yourself and in God. Stay on your knees, be generous, do service as much as you can, keep in touch with your family and friends—those things keep your spirit going. I try to keep a positive attitude because I know that any time you devote yourself to something, you will eventually reap the benefits of it.

I come from a poor family so we didn't have a lot of money. I was a teenager before we finally got a television. As a child, I was very introverted. I thought I was ugly, and I was really into books. I was this little skinny kid with big eyes and this little tiny voice. When you have those kinds of problems you deal with them by thinking, *I'm going to be big one day!*

The women of my family, especially my mom and my grandmother, really shaped my life. They were very strong. They taught me that the best thing we can do for children is to let them be whatever they want to be, to get out of their way and let them through! I had a lot of people around me who loved me and helped me blossom. My mother used to read poetry to me. From her poetry reading, I realized how much I liked drama and performance. I became one of the key singers in my church. I had this incredibly high voice so they used to just point to me, and I would hit a high note. In high school I got into drama, and I went on to study theater in college.

After I graduated, I worked in Houston as the artistic director of the Black Arts Center. For a long time I taught community theater. I was teaching everybody how to perform based on what I had learned as an undergraduate, but along the way I discovered that I really wanted to be an actress myself. I felt that I had to go to New York or somewhere or I would never get to do it, so I went to graduate school at Brandeis University to study drama. After I finished, I got a part in *Hair* on Broadway, and I have worked in show business ever since.

My big break in theater was as part of the original cast of *Dream Girls,* which was revolutionary for everybody. It was a big, long-running hit during the '80s, and I was in it for over four years. I think *Dream Girls* changed the look of Black women in this country. Diana Ross always did the big hair, but after *Dream Girls,* the whole glamorous face, long hair, and nails became the rave for everyday Black women. The same thing happened in *Waiting to Exhale,* which was my big break in film. It put me on the map. All those heavier women were so excited to see themselves on the screen in a positive light. After all, I was *not* the one who ended up alone—I got to be with Gregory Hines. Women still come up and say, "Oh, thank you. Thank you." And you think, *Oh my God, is it this important?* Because it seems like it shouldn't be, but it had a lot to do with women's self-esteem. Now, I realize it with my self. When I see women of color on television or in film, I celebrate because it is important and it makes me proud, so I understand how I can make others feel the same pride. I have been so lucky in that way. I have been in the stuff that changes the world!

I make sure to enjoy my successes because I go through a lot of rejection. That still happens to me, but I audition constantly. The problem is that there are not a lot of great roles to audition for, especially in my age group. When you get into your forties, it is just a different reality. When I started out, I thought the sky was the limit. I didn't understand that there was a ceiling on things because this business is so fickle. At the same time, I have been getting a chance to do the types of roles that I have never been asked to play before. I have always been a character actress so I was always the one on the side, the one who's the friend of the leading lady. But I am starting to do more leading lady roles, which is really exciting for me, especially at this stage of my career.

Actors are associated with a certain amount of fantasy. They get to do things that for others, are not legally or morally justified. Married men who are actors get to kiss a lot of different women. Single women get to pretend that they are married. You get to play a doctor on television, when you really know nothing about medicine. Anything you wanted to be or to accomplish is possible. There is so much magic and mysticism around actors, and I think some actors get caught up in it.

I think that what a lot of actors need to do is to stay connected to normal people, who can tone them down a bit. Because if you are a successful actor, and you are working consistently, you need something to tie your string to. Otherwise, you can blow away. That's what happens to a lot of people in this business. I have a lot of things that I love to do. I like sewing. My grandmother taught me to sew so I make a lot of things, and you can see me wearing things that I designed and created myself. I'm learning how to make jewelry, to sculpt and do a lot of other artsy stuff. I pray a lot. I read a lot, especially books about keeping the spirit awake. I think those kinds of things help me stay connected to what I value. That's how I make sure that all of the changes that happen in the industry don't change how I feel about myself and how I feel about the things and the people I love.

Acting is a wonderful experience. It's a wonderful life as long as you can really get in there and enjoy it. There are highs to it that I don't think can be matched by anything else that happens on this earth. I know that acting has been the right choice for me. I have been really blessed. There are so many talented people, so many people who must have prayed for it as hard as I did. I have been so lucky because I keep getting to work in the profession that I love. I am definitely blessed, but now, if they would pay me a bunch of money, I would be super, super blessed!

lena horne

dignity

---

*Dignity is something that no one can take away from you. In the
beginning it was a challenge for every Black person I'd ever known
just to exist. And we were proud we did. I'm proud to be an artist.
I'm proud to be a great grandmother. The thing I'm most proud of is
living. I'm glad I existed. I'm glad I survived.*

i was raised by very old-fashioned people who were Black and proud of it. We
were proud of all the Black people who came before me. That's the kind of raising
I had. My grandmother was an activist, and she taught me a lot about the impor-
tance of standing up for yourself and for your people.

I think that background is what made me feel so angry about the racism we all
endured. But it also gave me the courage to speak out even when it got me into trouble and to fight even when I knew I might lose. I learned that even if we couldn't
have our rights and we couldn't have our way, we could still have our pride. Dignity
is something that no one can take away from you. They may try—honey, they *will*
try—but you don't have to let them.

When I was younger, I wasn't interested in show business. I wanted to be a
schoolteacher. I wanted to read, travel, and lead a much more private life. But I
had to help support my family. When I was sixteen, I started working at The Cot-
ton Club in Harlem. I was just happy to have a job and be able to feed my mother.
At that time, I was inspired by the people who were stars there: Cab Calloway, Bil-
lie Holiday, Jimmy Lunsford, Ethel Waters, Adelaide Hall.

One day, someone from MGM saw me and liked my performing so I became
the first Black woman to have a contract with a major studio. At that time, the

NAACP saw me as someone who could clear a path to improve the way our people were represented so I moved to Hollywood. I remember when I went in to talk to the studio, I was so nervous I brought my father with me. My father was a very handsome and elegant man, the kind of Black man who Hollywood pretended did not exist. I was very proud to have him with me. Daddy told Louis B. Mayer, who was the head of MGM, that under no circumstances would his daughter be playing a maid or any undignified roles in any of their movies. Now, my image was also under the protection of the various Black organizations that had encouraged me to come to Hollywood so the studios knew that they were being watched very closely. So they didn't make me play any maids, but they didn't let me play anything else either.

During World War II, I got into trouble on the MGM tour because I didn't like the way they were treating the Black soldiers and I wouldn't sing unless they allowed Black soldiers to be part of the audience. At one point they even seated a group of White men they said were German POWs in front of the Black soldiers. I made a lot of noise about this, and I filed a complaint with the local NAACP so MGM pulled me off the tour. But I kept on touring and singing for Black soldiers on my own.

During the McCarthy Era, in the early '50s, I was black-listed in red channels and wasn't allowed to work for seven years on radio or in television. They said it was because I was a Communist since I was friends with Paul Robeson. But it was really because I was an activist, because I spoke out against racial injustice, and they wanted to keep me quiet.

One day I was in a restaurant, and this man called me a racially insulting word. You know the one. Well, honey, I threw everything I could get my hands on at that man—ashtrays, lamps, everything. Word got out about it, and I guess that's when everyone started to realize how serious I was about my beliefs.

I read and I saw so many things that changed me and the way I understood things. I saw how Martin Luther King, Jr., James Baldwin, and, later, even Malcolm X had learned to fight and forgive at the same time. Because I saw so many white people working together with us and because the message of the movement was one of forgiveness, I started to let go of some of my rage. Instead, I started to feel proud of all of us, of what we were standing for, and of what we were able to achieve.

But it wasn't until I did my Broadway show in 1981 that I realized the toll that all of that anger had taken on me, personally. When I sang on stage for a lot of my career, I was so furious about segregation and so determined to defy their images of Black women that I became unreachable. It was something that I had always done just to survive as a Black woman in this country. I put up walls to protect myself, but, in some ways, I also ended up locking myself in. When I did my Broadway show, I finally let those walls down. I let everyone see who I really am. They accepted me, and I accepted myself. I'd been singing all my life, but in that show I felt like I had finally found my voice.

The best advice I ever received came from my father, who didn't want me to be obligated to anyone. He said I had to work hard and pay for what I got.

we only survived because we all depended on each other. Back then, it was still one of each. Only one. One got a favor. One was a jazz singer. One sang the white songs that they heard the white stars sing. One was a ballet dancer. Well, honey, I learned firsthand that the "only one" system doesn't really work. It doesn't really change anything. That's why it was so important during the civil rights movement for us to all stand together to make things happen. If we had kept doing things one at a time, we never would have gotten anywhere.

If I could have started my career over again, I would have started it in better times. I would have loved to have had it like it is now with the way young Black people are. They get rich; they're in business, they're CEOs; they have computers. It's a whole new generation. I can't compare my experience to any of it.

I have a family now. That's what I'm proud of. I'm proud of my grandchildren. I have no brothers or sisters, and I have lost so many people whom I've loved. But now, I have a great, great grandson, and I never expected that! In the beginning, it was a challenge for every Black person I'd ever known just to exist. I'm proud to be an artist. I'm proud to be a great-grandmother. The thing I'm most proud of is living. I'm glad that I existed. I'm glad that I survived.

boris kodjoe

discernment

*I don't settle for less. I don't choose the easy route. I turn down more
things than I accept because I don't want to do things that would
compromise who I am and what I'm trying to do.*

i have always put more than 100 percent into what I do, first in tennis, then in
modeling, and now in acting. I have always put discipline and determination first
when it came to work. All of my experiences have taught me lessons, and I tried
to take as much as I could from those experiences, those lessons, and from the
choices I have made.

I have a vision. I have a goal, and I'm always in the process of slowly approaching that goal. I don't settle for less. I don't choose the easy route. I turn
down more things than I accept because I don't want to do things that would compromise who I am and what I'm trying to do. That's the way to come out happier—
to wake up in the morning, look myself in the eye, and smile.

I grew up in Germany. My father's from Ghana, West Africa, and my mom is
German. My mother had a tremendous influence on my life because she made
me confident as a young Black person growing up in white Germany, which was
not always the easiest thing. I remember very clearly telling my parents that I
wanted to be a professional tennis player. From the time I was three years old,
tennis was my life. I became one of the top three players in Germany and went
professional when I was sixteen. Then, when I was eighteen, I had back problems
so I decided that it was too risky to pursue tennis exclusively. I decided to accept
a scholarship to study in the United States and get my college degree.

When I was still in school, and on a visit to New York, this lady named Rita Valentine came up to me and gave me her card. She asked me what agency I was with, but I told her I wasn't interested in modeling because I was still in college. After I graduated, I visited New York again. I called Rita up, and she told me, "Well, there's this great photographer who lives two blocks away from where you are staying, so why don't you go see him?" That person was fashion photographer Bruce Weber.

I had no idea about fashion modeling, but I went over and met the guy. He was really cool. He asked me if I had anything to do the next day, and I said no. He said, "Okay, I have this job and you would be perfect for it." So the next day I had my first job, which was for Versace with Bruce Weber. I had an apartment a week later, and that's when my career took off.

Rita became my booker at the Ford Modeling Agency. She had a vision for me—a long-term vision. She presented me to clients as a high-profile model as opposed to somebody who would just do anything for any amount of money. Often, in the fashion industry, people get thrown out right and left. You make a quick buck, and then you're gone. She really looked out for me. I owe her everything in terms of my modeling career because from the beginning she had a very serious interest in me as a person and she wanted the best for me.

I learned a lot from modeling, but I had been interested in acting since I was about thirteen years old, maybe even younger. It was just a matter of time before I actually pursued it. I love the process of acting. It's so refreshing to be able to be expressive, to have your mind stimulated. You forget that when you do something like modeling, where your intellectual abilities are not necessarily appreciated. Modeling gave me the resources and the freedom to act. I moved to Los Angeles and got an agent. I went to auditions and, for the first time, I had to get used to being turned down.

As soon as I got to Los Angeles, I started studying, educating myself. I went to class all the time and worked hard on my skills and my speech. Acting class is very necessary because you have to know who you are before you can dig into other characters. You have to be in control of who you are. In our society, you have to portray so many different characters in daily life who are so far away from your true being that it can be very tough to find your way back to yourself.

You have to get to know yourself and let go of all your preconceived notions about youself, of all the pressures you feel people put on you to act in a certain way. You have to learn how to let all of that go, to let all those walls fall down and to totally expose yourself. That's a very grueling, very painful process sometimes, but I think it's important. Then everything else is like any other job you do. It involves a lot of studying and a lot of training. The more you do, the more skilled you become.

The best advice anyone ever gave me about modeling was to tell me that nothing is the way it looks, that the whole thing is a lot of hype, so I had to watch my back. Everybody's very nice to you. Especially when you go from zero to the top, everybody loves you. They're offering you things and inviting you everywhere. That's an amazing temptation. And it's very dangerous. It is important to be careful about who you trust and who you follow. It's kind of wild and exciting in the beginning when you see your own billboard towering above you, and people are running up to you, wanting to take their picture with you. But that thrill wears off, and you realize that it's just the picture and not you that they're interested in. Those people don't really care about you. They just care about who you are. You have to be close to your friends, to your *real* friends, and to your family. I always had contact with my family on a daily basis, and I think that kept me on the right path.

I always urge people who are interested in modeling to finish their education first. I try to open everybody's eyes to that because modeling is not always a pleasant business. It's full of temptations, dangers, and people who cannot always be trusted. So if you are interested in modeling, do what you have to do in your life, especially in terms of education. Then, when you have a minute and want to travel and see the world, you can pursue modeling because it provides that opportunity. You travel, you make some money, and you meet a lot of interesting people. If you're a strong person you can just take the best out of it and move on. That's why I say to finish your education first, because that usually means you're at an age where you're mature enough to handle the temptations, pressures, and whatever else is placed in your path.

I'm very excited about the future, and I'm very focused. I'm totally concentrating on the art, on trying to become a better actor. I'm not really worried about what's going on beside me or next to me. I'm not concerned with the politics of the industry. I'm just trying to become better at everything I do.

star jones

encouragement

You have got to tell your children that they are the best thing since swinging doors. Because you know what? They will grow up, and they will believe it.

i've always been encouraged to go for it and to believe in myself. My confidence is born of a place in my heart. It's always been in me. It was a gift given to me a long time ago. The women in my family, and the men in my family, have always given me that support and encouragement. Whenever I give advice, it is not really advice to the child. It is advice to the parent. The advice is—you have got to tell your children that they are the best thing since swinging doors. Because you know what? They will grow up, and they will believe it.

I knew then as I know now that God had a divine purpose for me on this earth. I'm still discovering it. I haven't accomplished everything that I wanted to or everything He set out for me to do, but I promise you, I'll make God proud. I'll do everything I'm supposed to do.

I've always wanted to be a lawyer. I never went through ballerina, teacher, astronaut, or Indian chief. I never wanted to be anything else. Once when I was a little girl, my grandmother and I were watching her favorite TV soap opera. There was a character, Rachel, who was always in trouble. I remember my grandmother saying, "That strumpet needs a lawyer!" I asked, "What's a lawyer?" She told me, "A lawyer is somebody who helps people and gets them out of trouble." So I said, "Well, I'm going to be a lawyer." And she said, "You can be whatever you want to be, baby." So of course, she told my mother, and my mother said, "Go for it." My grandmother had no higher education because she was raising a family. My

mother had a college education. But their response to their little Black child wanting to become a lawyer was to go for it! That really kind of set the stage for who I am and how I got here. So I set off on my path and eventually became a successful prosecutor.

I started doing television when I did some legal commentary for *Court TV*. I didn't have a trial that week, which is the only reason why I did it, and that experience changed my life. I wanted people to know that the law was theirs and that it could be user-friendly if you just understood it. And I wanted to prove that an African-American woman could command attention and respect. People had never seen a young African-American woman break down the law with that level of confidence before. From there, I became a full-time television legal correspondent and eventually hosted my own show, called *Jones & Jury*.

Today, I love my work. The four things I love to do are talk, express my opinion, hang with my girl friends, and dress up. *The View* provides me with an opportunity to do all four every single day. When people ask me, "Do you miss being in front of a jury?" I say, "All I've done is trade in one jury for another." But this one just happens to be a jury of millions.

My education is the foundation for all I have achieved. I would not be on television every day if I did not have a law degree and a college degree. Even as a child, I knew education could free you from difficult economic and social circumstances. Education is the foundation for everything. Wherever I go, I always feel like I belong there. Regardless of my skin color, regardless of my gender, regardless of anything about my physical self, I belong there! I have a good sense of self and that came from my family and from my education. But I've also worked very hard on it.

I believe that short-term decisions have long-term ramifications so I set short-term goals and work on them every single day. I also take chances. You've got to be willing to fly without a net sometimes. I have never taken no for an answer. I don't know what the words "can't" or "don't" mean. I'm not the kind of person who would walk over you if you were in my way. But I'll figure out a way around you, and I always have.

I am still following my original path. If you talk to people who have known me all of my life, they will tell you, "Star is the exact same person she was when she was four. She just has more money and dresses better." I know not to put ice-blue eye shadow on, but I am the same exact person! I know who I am. And no amount of press, politics, or bad words are ever going to change how I feel about me. I'm too far gone. Nothing is going to ever get me down. I have always had a good sense of self. That comes from my family, but I've also worked very hard on it.

When I first started with *The View*, I was concerned because I'm not your typical media version of a Black woman. I don't apologize for being who I am. I don't apologize for being full-figured, for being brown-skinned, for changing my hair every other day. I don't apologize for being smart or for coming from a family who loves me. I don't apologize for being Christian and very pro-choice, for not liking animals and for not being sure if I want children. I don't apologize for thinking that I'm beautiful. One time I met Diahann Carrol, one of my lifelong idols since childhood, and told her these things. I said, "I'm just not sure that they're ready for me." And her response was, "They had better get ready!" And I thought to myself, *She's right!* It was the best advice anybody could have ever given me and I will value it for the rest of my life.

The most important thing to do is to fill our children with a sense of self, to let them know that they have options, that there are *no* doors they cannot open. I want little girls out there to realize that you don't have to apologize for who you are. You're not allowed to be arrogant, but you *are* allowed to be confident. You are not allowed to put other people down, but you *are* allowed to lift yourself up. I worry about those little girls who were not given the foundation of love and support that I was given because somebody could penetrate their souls and get to them. I want to teach them not to have a hardened heart, but to have a heartened heart. It's heartened because you know who you are. Maybe there is some little girl out there who is saying, "You know, Star Jones accomplished this. I can, too!" For me, that is about as good as it gets.

samuel l. jackson

endurance

I was very fortunate that fame didn't come until I'd learned to do a whole lot of different things. The work is what makes me happy. It never occurred to me to quit. From early on, it was instilled in me that it was about the work and not the result of the work.

the best piece of advice I ever heard was that luck is the perfect meeting of preparation and opportunity. You always stay prepared so that when opportunity knocks, you're ready to open that door—and step through it.

I was very fortunate that fame didn't come until I'd learned to do a lot of different things. When somebody sees me work, they see the accumulation of all the things that I've learned to do—how to break down a character and look inside of it, how to ask myself the right questions about what's going on in a particular scene or moment so that I can make that clear to an audience and have dramatic impact. That's all the result of hard work, preparation, good training, and understanding my role as an actor—doing the job.

I believe that every job is a path or stepping-stone to something else. There is always something to be learned, no matter how small or large the role is. I don't have problems with the work. The work is what makes me happy. That's the joyous thing, to be able to do the work and to have no trepidation about it. I'm always looking forward to it.

When I was in the Drama Department at Morehouse College, we had professors who encouraged us to go out and get agents and see what the business was like. They encouraged us to see the reality of the business. Not just the fantasy. But most of all, we were taught that the important things were perseverance and effort, going about the business of learning to be the best at what you do.

From early on, it was instilled in me that it was about the work and not about the result of the work so that was basically how I had to approach what I was doing. Then things just happened. Success was never the goal of what I was doing. I was actually always more concerned about the work itself, and I still am in a very definite kind of way. I'm being honest for an audience. I'm being honest to myself. I'm being true to the character, and I'm conveying the information that the writer wanted to give to the audience. That's about it for me. All the rest of this stuff just kind of happens.

I struggled, but I never worried about whether or not it was worth it. Acting was what I was doing and what I wanted to do. It was just about working wherever I could. I did a lot of bus and trucks, a lot of tours. I always found a way to work. When I wasn't acting, I was building sets and hanging lights and doing something in the theater.

It never occurred to me to quit. Everybody I knew was doing theater, and that's what my wife, LaTonya, and I did, so it wasn't about doing something else. Everybody wants things to happen at the exact time that they want them to. But I've always been very accepting of what's going on around me. I wasn't trying to be a movie star, or to be famous, or to be anything way before it was supposed to happen. I was trying to be an actor.

I watched people leave to do what they were doing. I was around when Morgan Freeman was around, when Denzel Washington was around, when Wesley Snipes was around, and you see other people break out. Then, every now and then, a break comes for you. That's the one thing that you can't be taught about this business. Being in the right place at the right time when things happen. I happened to be there, and Spike Lee wanted to work with me, and *Jungle Fever* kind of happened at the right place and at the right time in my career. That performance and the awards I received for it got me into Hollywood. They started wondering, who is *this* guy? So that was a big break, but breaks are things you define in different kinds of ways. You have to define them in terms of how they shape your life and how they change the way you see yourself, not just in terms of how they change the way others see you.

The reality of success is actually a lot bigger than the dream. Your career will lead you to all kinds of things that you can't predict. One day, you're doing theater at the Negro Ensemble Company, and you're in a dressing room with ten other people putting on your makeup. At that time, it's hard to imagine being in a trailer just for you that's bigger than that entire ten-person dressing room or being on location and making more in per diem than you made as a salary when you were working in theater. Those kinds of things don't cross your mind as you're trying to succeed. You can't imagine people getting speechless, hyperventilating, losing it, and doing all kinds of crazy stuff when they meet you. It's an incredible thing. When my family was on vacation in Italy, we were walking around the Vatican with the other tourists, and a priest stopped us and said, "Oh my God! It's Samuel L. Jackson!" It's like, Damn! I must be famous!

The most intriguing thing for me is what is going to happen in my daughter Zoe's life. I think about how she'll be and how it's really great that we've been able to create a good life for her. We hope she'll find something that's important to her and that she enjoys doing, something that intrigues her, that sparks her interest, that will allow her to be an important member of society.

We influence young people through what we do and not just by what we say. The most important way we can inspire young people is by succeeding at the things we do, by showing them that there are viable career opportunities, and by creating spaces through what we do. Often people don't view the arts as a viable career choice, but through the way that we succeed, talk about it, and continue to be out there, we can encourage young people to pursue the things that they want to pursue, believe in their dreams, and work hard to make them come true.

robert townsend

enthusiasm

True success is going from failure to failure without any loss of enthu-siasm. Success is conquering fear. Each time you take a chance and you have fun, you forget about the fear and keep moving.

to dare to dream means going into the unknown and embracing it. Whatever people think, they think. But you have to embrace what *you* think is funny or dra-matic or touching and go with it. Don't second-guess yourself. Keep moving.

Anybody who's pursuing a dream needs to know that failure comes with it. Sometimes you have to hit a wall to understand certain things before you can go on. The bottom line is that failure is a necessary brick on the road to success. True success is going from failure to failure without any loss of enthusiasm. Because at least you've tried, even when things don't go the way you want them to go. I am always proud to say that at least I tried. There are so many people who are so afraid to even try. But some of the most successful people started on one path, hit a wall, and then were able to regroup and turn things around so that they became successful.

anytime you're going to do something different, and you step out there, there's always a certain amount of fear because you're going into the unknown. I'm go-ing to try something that hasn't been tried before. I'm going to do something that hasn't been done. It's safe to just do what you know, but all my movies have been different and all my television shows have been different. That makes it even harder for me. But each time you take a chance, and you have fun—you forget about the fear and keep moving.

Success is conquering fear. You have to step out there and take chances. Successful people continue to take chances and try different things. I think that's what it's about. It's like the song in *The Five Heartbeats:* "No matter how hard it gets, we haven't finished yet."

television had the biggest impact on me because my mother raised four kids on her own. So sometimes when she wasn't there because she was working, the television was the babysitter. I learned a lot about life and got a reinforcement about values and morals from television. My nickname as a kid was "TV Guide" because I used to watch everything on TV and I could do impressions of everyone. So my friends said, "Hey, man, you should be acting." I think that's what kind of started it. I won my first award in 1968 when I was at a high school speech festival. And one of my first English teachers, Mr. James Reed, was the one who encouraged me to really pursue it. I think that's when it started for me as a kid.

Directing really came out of my frustration of auditioning for the same kind of roles and my wanting to do something different. I just said, "Hey, the director really controls the movie and really creates the movie. The actor is there, but it's really the director who has the power." I think learning to direct is like learning anything else. You study and you learn a technique, and you study directors whose work you love. It's just a hunger that comes over you when you want to learn something.

My biggest break would have to be *Hollywood Shuffle*, definitely. I did that film for a quarter of a million dollars, and I shot it in only twelve days. That is very unusual for a feature film. In addition to being able to work with extremely limited resources, I think that the film really showed that I had an understanding of the camera and storytelling. It was a lot of hard work, but it was a lot of fun.

I'm an outsider, and I'm an insider. I began as a rebel. I've done things that are still on the rebel cusp, but I've worked mainstream. It's really about the material. Can you do the kinds of projects that you want to do? I think that's really what it's about. For me, there are days I feel like an outsider because Hollywood makes the same kinds of films all of the time, and if you want to make something different, you have to have another kind of mindset. You have days when you fight with the studio. You have days when you tussle with the actors, days when the script doesn't work. But that's all par for the course. In the end, it's always worth the struggle.

i think it's great to be around minds that think like you think—positively. But you can also easily be around negative minds that can drag you down. When I was an extra, there were a lot of extras that were, like, "Hey, man, when you become an extra that's all you're ever going to be." If you buy into that, you'll never get anywhere. Those are the only people who can kill your dream, people who are closest to you. I just think that if you surround yourself with positive people and people who believe in your dream, you'll always win.

The person I always looked up to was Sidney Poitier. He was the first African-American man I ever saw on television who had dignity. I remember the first time I met him. I asked him, "How did you have such dignity in those movies back then in the fifties when there were all those demeaning stereotypes?" And he said, "I chose to use the power of 'no.' That's the one power I did have in my control. I didn't have to do every role. I said 'no.' I've never forgotten that."

I will always cherish how my career began, despite the difficulties. I consider myself blessed. I am totally blessed to make movies and television, blessed by the fact that I've been able to write, direct, produce, and act in movies and television shows. I have a job that I love going to, that I love doing. So I think that in itself is a blessing. I would like to be remembered for creating an incredible body of work that affected people in a good way—work that made them laugh, made them cry, but more importantly, made them think, and, I hope, made the planet just a little bit better.

The best advice I ever got was to always keep God first. And it works. It works. It is exciting these days that everyone's continuing to work and trying to create some great work. That's what it's all about. The sky's the limit.

tommy davidson

faith

*If I looked at, judged, and weighed all the circumstances that were
lined up against me and against my success, then I would fail every
time. I grow by faith, not by sight.*

every day is a struggle. Every day, it is darkest before the dawn. But you can
only transition from the dark into the light if you continue to have faith. I grow by
faith, not by sight. If I looked at, and judged, and weighed all the circumstances
that were lined up against me and against my success, then I would fail every
time. My belief in myself and God has made me cross that bridge every time I
come to it. It's a constant challenge just to remain faithful—to remain faithful and
to believe.

Sometimes it's a struggle to just have enough confidence in myself to accept
all of the good things that I have. Sometimes I become uninspired because I'm a
very emotional person, and when things don't go exactly the way I would like
them to go, I can spiral down. That's where that faith part comes in. No matter
what comes my way, I know that everything is going to be okay. Sometimes I have
to work my way into that kind of thinking. Faith is the toughest challenge. It affects
every aspect of who I am. Faith is that quiet and still part of who I am—the part of
me that is helping me fulfill my goals.

I was born in Greenfield, Mississippi, but I grew up in Maryland, right over the
DC line. I was born in 1963, and I was adopted in 1965. My adoption was a result
of the civil rights movement, which was at its peak at the time. My natural mom,
who was Black, was working in the movement and so was my mother who raised
me, who was White. My adoption was kind of a sign of the times.

My mom had the most influence on my life. She provided me with all the information that I needed to get cool with the way that the world is. For a while when I was a kid, I got involved in a lot of things that I should have stayed away from. I think what turned my life around was getting a job. The minute that I was exposed to people who had different types of survival skills, I changed. Having a job instilled in me the idea that I can actually determine my own destiny by working toward it both physically and mentally.

I got started in comedy when a friend of mine asked me to try stand-up in a club in Washington, DC where he worked. I went there one night and tried it, and I haven't looked back. I've been basically doing that ever since. Stand-up led to my moving from DC to Hollywood, which led to doing stand-up here, which led to television, which led to films.

The toughest challenge for me when I first began was to make the transition from being an everyday worker to making a living being an entertainer. It took about three years to make that transition. I was working at a delicatessen, and finally, one day, I made as much money working as an MC and playing at clubs as I did at the deli. I told my supervisor at the job that I was quitting, and I walked out. I had actually started making a living doing comedy. That was the moment that I crossed over. That was a milestone for me because it was like walking out onstage. It was believing that I could do it.

Robert Townsend gave me one of my first major opportunities. He put me on Robert Townsend's *Partners in Crime*, which was a very popular show on HBO at the time. It was my first national exposure, and it really helped my career a lot. He was one of the first people I credit with discovering my talent and putting me in a place where everyone else could see it.

A new, young comedian who moves to Los Angeles should find out where the first open mike is. There are clubs out here where you can go onstage for free. You get on a list, and you go and work your material. I would try to get seven days at seven different clubs each week where I could go and work on my stuff. The way I learned the business aspect of this business was to ask questions and seek knowledge. There are people who will help you, talk to you, and share information with you, and there are people who won't. When you can't get the information from others, you have to go and seek the information for yourself. You have to do the research and educate yourself, which is what I did. I continue to educate myself about the business side. It's very difficult because there is always something new to learn. Having the knowledge isn't enough. You have to be able to put the knowledge into action. It's one thing to say that you want to do something. It's another thing to lay out a plan—which is work in itself—and actually follow through with every step of that plan. That's probably the most difficult part, but it's also provided me with the most growth of my career.

Every aspect of my life—and every person who touches my life—influences me as a person. The janitor who is mopping up the hallway can influence me just as much as a director of a major motion picture. The chain of events that have led to this moment in time, all of them, have shaped me into the person who I am, and I like who I am right now. I'm living the kind of life where I'm actually becoming who I want to be as I speak, as I walk, as I breathe, as I think. One of the things that's really, really cool about my life is that I'm an artist, which means that I get to share my perceptions and my creativity with other people. There's no dollar value that you can put on that. There's no mathematical equation. There are no re-straints. There are no rules. That is a gift from God. To be a part of the same world as Picasso, Beethoven, Spike Lee, James Baldwin, Shakespeare—to be an artist is to be one of those people. I like that. I like that a lot.

gordon parks

fearlessness

People could do many things if they just tried, but they're afraid. I have always had a great desire and curiosity about the world and what you can accomplish in it. At times, I have been afraid, but I have never allowed fear to stand in my way.

in my life, I've learned important things about my choice of weapons in the fight against bigotry, discrimination, and poverty. It was fortunate that I didn't choose the gun or the knife because a lot of my friends lost their way and their lives by taking that route. My weapon turned out to be the camera. At the same time, I've always believed that poetry should be in everything I do, no matter what the medium or the subject. It should be in my music. It should be in my literature. It should be in my photography and my films. Everything should involve poetry.

I think that many people could do many things if they just tried, but they're afraid. They want to write a novel, but they're afraid to try to write a novel. They want to play music, but they're afraid to try. I don't attach any genius to what I've done. I think that in many ways, I was just trying to survive. All of the things that I've done are things that I really found tremendously interesting. That's what I do when I get bored or restless, I turn towards something new. I have always had a great desire and curiosity about the world and what you can accomplish in it. At times, I have been afraid, but I have never allowed fear to stand in my way.

I'm from a little town called Fort Scott, Kansas. You have to be careful when you approach it because if you don't look up quickly, you may miss it. But that was home until I was fifteen years old. My family all wanted me to be something that I was afraid I couldn't be. But I tried. They're all deceased now. But they're

still here for me. And when I've needed them most, the spirit of them was always there.

My mother would not allow me to complain about what I was denied because I was Black. Her idea was, and her words were, "If a white boy can do it, you can do it, and you'd better do it better, or don't come home." So I listened to what Sara Parks said. She said, "Don't mind what other people are doing. Do what you have to do. Ignore other people if they try to stop you. You must have confidence in yourself." My father backed her up. He was a rather gentle man. He was a dirt farmer, but he kept us alive and that was what was important. My mother died when I was fifteen. She wanted me sent to Minnesota away from the more obvious discrimination so I went to live there with an older sister.

When I was about nineteen years old, I was a waiter on the railway. In between runs, the others went out on the town looking for ladies, but I would go to the movies. One day I saw a newsreel about a photographer named Norman Alley who was recognized for bravery during the war. Then they said, "Norman Alley is in the theater!" He jumped out on stage in a white suit so I thought that he must have a very glamorous job. That inspired me, so when I got to Seattle, Washington, I bought my first camera at a pawnshop. I think it was about $12.50. It was a terrible camera. That afternoon, I shot film for the first time and fell into the Puget Sound trying to photograph seagulls. When I got back to Minneapolis, I showed my film to the Eastman Kodak people, and they thought it was a good start. They told me that if I kept it up, they'd give me a show. And they did. I started doing fashion photography and I received a fellowship to work with the Foreign Security Administration in Washington.

Roy Stryker was the head of the FSA. He was my mentor as a photographer, my guiding light. He was not a photographer, but he was in charge of a photography project under Franklin Roosevelt. Some of the most important documentary photographers of our time were working there when I was sent there to train with him. He was very particular about where we should point the camera and how we should treat people when we did. I'll never forget him. He was instrumental in pointing me in the right direction. That experience eventually led to work I did for *Vogue* and *Life* magazines, where they had never before hired Black photographers.

I think I was probably endowed with musical talent from the very beginning because I was playing the piano when I was six years old, although I never studied. I was working in Paris as a photographer for *Life* when I met Dean Dixon, a black orchestra conductor. He came to visit me one day, and he heard me playing piano. When I was through playing, he came in and he said, "What was that?" And I said, "Oh, that was my first piano concerto." I'd been to Spain, and I'd seen a bullfighter killed by a bull. It was on my mind and all coming out in my fingers. I told him I was kidding, but he was serious. He said, "You put it on tape, and we'll ship it back to America and have it orchestrated. I'm going to perform it in Venice and I want you to be there." That's the way that happened. But before that particular moment, I would never believe that I could put together a piano concerto with four movements.

I got into directing after John Cassavetes, who was a very well-known actor and later a director, had read my first novel, *The Learning Tree,* which was about growing up in Kansas. He called from Hollywood and he said, "I read your book last night, and it would make one hell of a movie. And you should direct it!" I said, "There aren't any Black directors in Hollywood, and there aren't going to be any." He said, "I don't know about that." He told me to come out and visit him at Warner Bros., and I went. Cassavetes introduced me to Kenny Hyman. Hyman and I talked about the film. He told me I could direct it, write the screenplay, and compose the score and Warner Bros. would produce it. Well, I didn't believe a word he said until I saw the news flashed across America that I was going to direct his film.

My favorite moment as a director was when they lifted me on that crane in the air and I said, "Roll 'em." The only thing beneath me was the Kansas prairie where I was born. Over to the left I could see the graveyard where my mother and father were buried in segregated graves. And here I was with a big crew, all the way from Hollywood, directing this movie. That was the biggest and most exciting moment for me.

I'm not particularly proud of being the first Black photographer for *Vogue* and *Life* magazines or of being the first Black director for a studio. I think it should have happened long before I came around. Many young people with talent were denied that. So I accepted those opportunities, and I tried to make the most of it so I could sort of set a mark for those who were going to follow me. But I didn't feel particularly proud. I felt this should have happened long before I was born. All that talent was wasted. It was a waste to the world, actually. That should never have happened and we have to stop it from happening now and in the future.

I would give young people the good advice that my mother gave me—you can do it if you want to do it. Some of my own children have followed in my footsteps. Gordon, the oldest boy, directed *Superfly.* My son, David, and my daughter, Tony, are photographers. One of my grandsons, Gordon Parks III, wants to be a rap star. I have five great-grandchildren and five grandchildren, and they are all doing their thing.

I want to be remembered for whatever I've done toward helping humanity. I love people. People have returned their love for me and I'm grateful for that. So I hope to be remembered for whatever I've accomplished. I've tried to do it well, and that's the most important thing I can say about it.

russell simmons

focus

You have to stick to your dream. You have to focus. You have to go to work every day and have but one goal.

i am a creative entrepreneur. I get this great idea. I get excited. I go to work on it. Then the hard work starts, and my idea moves very slowly a lot of times, slower than you'd expect. It always seems very slow to me. At the end of the day you're struggling to promote something or develop something that no one sees but you—that's what everybody has to get past. That's the point where people give up, and that to me is the critical point of developing any idea into a business.

you really have to know that there are going to be a lot of times when people will question what you're doing and when you're going to question yourself. But if you had that gut feeling in the beginning, and there's something there, and you give up—you're going to regret it. Usually it takes years before people accept you. It took years of my giving parties and working toward being in the record industry before I got a record out. And then it took seven years before my clothing business took off. People forget it's not often an overnight success. They don't know. It has to do with a real focus, and a real hard-work ethic, and a singular kind of attitude about what you are trying to get done. You have to stick to your dream. You have to go to work every day and have but one goal.

my father had the most impact on me while I was growing up. He inspired me to focus and to work hard on my focus.

My interest in the entertainment business is something that developed when I was in college. I think going to college, just having that experience, allows you to dream. College is one of the best places for people to formulate plans. It really is a place where people make those decisions and where they get an opportunity to see a lot as they make those decisions. The most freedom you have is when you're in college. It's the one time you really believe that you can do things, and it's the first time you can really dream about those things. College is where I started to formulate expectations for my future—and a plan.

It started with giving parties. That's how I learned that young people are always looking for great music with great energy and that they are willing to pay to listen and dance to it. Giving parties was more of an entrepreneurial thing. Later, I translated that same idea of making people feel like they were part of something exciting and unique into the record business. That's one of the things that hip-hop music does for people. It creates a community for them. I wanted to be involved in building that community from the streets up. I was always going to clubs and stuff and promoting parties. It became my source of income, and it also became a passion because the music was hip-hop. There were no hip-hop records yet, but the industry, the artists, and the music became my passion through my giving parties.

The first record I was involved in was Kurtis Blow's "Christmas Rapping," which came out in 1979. Getting that first record out was the most difficult thing I did in those early years. They still play it every year, and it is considered one of the earliest hip-hop records.

We were doing the second Run-DMC album and I heard this record on the radio, "It's Yours." It was such a dope record. Rick Rubin produced it and Jazzy J introduced me to him. He was in the club Danceteria, where we used to always get our records played. He and the Beastie Boys produced this record, and he'd put it out independently. He was just a college kid, but he was a great producer who was also an artist. We started working together, and I started managing the Beastie Boys and him. Then he asked if we could start a record company. I was already doing that with someone else, but he convinced me that it made sense. I actually put money up with him when we started a company, which was Def Jam. That was in 1984.

This is the communications business, first of all, which is critical. It means that in order to be successful, you must recognize, appreciate, and support talent. The talent you cultivate carries the image and the message that your business is sending out to the rest of the world. You need to be able to make connections and to make connections work for you, but you also need personal resources, which is something I think everybody has if they reach inside. That's why focus is so important. It makes it possible for you to bring a lot of different elements together and make them work.

Throughout my career, I was a manager at heart. I was a manager in theory, and in reality. I was a manager always. You have to have an appreciation of talent and be able to support that talent. The record company was formed because we needed to get artists' records out and promoted properly, and we needed the image of the artists represented properly. That control was the element that was lost through using other distributors, so for us to do our own ideas properly, we had to be independent.

In this respect, the film business is not different from the record business. What I did in each case early on was to find vehicles for the artists. All the rappers wanted to make movies. But Run-DMC, Kurtis Blow, and LL Cool J didn't have any movie vehicles so we created that for ourselves with *Krush Groove.*

The music industry is still a battle. The corporations—as much as they are supportive to some degree—realize that it's not their industry. They would prefer not to have to use hip-hop music and culture as a vehicle to promote their products. They don't like the way it has so much control and power. The fact is it does have that power, and I think that those of us who are part of creating hip-hop culture need to take our power seriously. We need to explore the possibilities it can create and the problems it can solve, especially for young people.

We can teach the next generation by example. You have to focus. You can't be all over the place. It may appear that I'm all over the place now because I'm involved in so many businesses, but the people around me are focused and hard-working and directed. You can't focus on too many things by yourself. In order to succeed, you need focus, hard work, and good communication skills.

I consider myself successful because I can pay my bills and do something I love at the same time. Where do I get my drive? It's passion. Passion drives me and focus gets me to my destination.

patti labelle

gratitude

You have to have gone through some hard times to really appreciate
things and not take them for granted once you get them. So I'm happy
that I have gone through a little hell.

what continues to drive me? Applause. Loving to be loved. That's it. To be wanted all the time and for people to really respect you. I love to please. That drives me. That's enough to keep you going and to keep you wanting to be out there. After you're home for a while you miss the live audience and the cheers, and even if you get booed, you miss that. Whatever the audience gives, I miss it, and it's enough to keep me going, knowing that they want me out there.

I am so blessed. It's just nice to be able to be in my position. I know my place. And I know that my place could be taken so that keeps my feet on the ground. I know that there are so many other women who have much more talent than I do who are still waiting in the wings. They just haven't had the chances that I've had. I never take my chances for granted.

Everything that I've gone through, the ups and downs, makes me appreciate all of the balance that I have now. I wouldn't have done it any other way. Because you have to have gone through some hard times to really appreciate things and not take them for granted once you get them. So I'm happy that I have gone through a little hell.

I was born and raised in Philadelphia. I was very influenced by my father as far as cooking, cleaning, and taking care of people. He was like the housewife, and he spoiled my mother. She can cook very well also. But my father was a chef. I just stayed in the kitchen, watching him cook. He was really a great, great father and

husband. I was influenced by my mother to be sassy. As he was cooking, she was sassing him, saying, "You better cook some more chicken."

My father sang very well so I was influenced by him and by my brother's choice of music. He listened to Nina Simone, Gloria Lynn, James Moody, Dakota Stayton, so those are the people who influenced me. I started by singing in the choir at church in Philadelphia. That's when I first came out as a solo performer. My choir director, Mrs. Harriet Chapman, made me sing solo because I was afraid to do anything in public, especially by myself. When I sang in the choir, that was fine because I had a lot of backup. But she forced me to do a solo one day, and the whole congregation stood up.

Then I just continued to be out there. After being in church choirs, I joined a singing group with three other ladies. When we had our first club gig, we had to split $50, and I got $10. I said, "Gosh, if we got ten dollars, we can get twenty next time." So that's when I said, "This mouth can make me a buck." From then on I started making $20, then $30 and then $40. We got a recording deal after that, and we became Patti LaBelle and the Bluebells in the 1960s. Then we performed for a while together, and the two ended up as three in the 70s, called Labelle. And then the rest is me. That's what's left.

Fame was never difficult for me. I've always handled it. I've never let it handle me. But when I started, I wasn't prepared to deal with the business side. All I wanted to do was to sing and look cute. I wanted to let my managers deal with the rest, and at the time I was hoping and trusting that they had my best interests at heart. I would tell people who are new to the business that you should try to have your business straight before you go into any new areas. So many things can be done to you in your name—things you may not even know about. You better get your education first. Know where your money is going and how much you are getting. Know who's counting it, and it better be you.

When I started out, the hardest thing to deal with was racism. Going to the back of restaurants or going to colored toilets or having to pee in a can. Today, the hardest part is still the racism. It's still in my face. It just doesn't bother me as much as it used to. In the future, it will be interesting to see if people will still be as ignorant as we are, to see if we will still be as crazy as we are. I'm hoping that we will change some spirits and some minds. I think it will change, eventually. I just hope I'm around when it does.

If you believe in yourself, just follow your dream. If you realize that you can sing, you should find somebody who is interested in your talent. Find somebody who is true and honest, which is very hard to do. Try to find a family member, if possible. When people tell you that you can't, just continue to believe that you can. So many people have been told "No. Get a real job. Do something else that you can do better." A lot of times, people can please a certain group of people and can't please another group, but the group that they are pleasing is the group that can put them on the map. You don't have to please everybody. You just have to connect with the people who want to help and support you.

The most important advice I ever received was to remember where you've come from. The other side of that is to remember where you are going. That means looking after all of our children because they are our future. We should all try to be decent role models for the children, because they have to have something to look forward to and someone to look up to. We have to look out for other people's children, not just our own, especially if they get out of line. They should know that they can look forward to getting a whupping from somebody if they do something wrong, no matter whose children they are. So if there are any out there messing around near me, I'm going to spank their butt. You can spank mine, too, if you see me doing wrong. I'm only human so I can still do wrong and I still will.

The most important thing to me now is being honest and being fair. I try not to be judgmental. I want to be remembered as someone who was as honest as I possibly could be. I want to be remembered as a giver—not a taker—because I love giving. I love to nurture or put a smile on your face or bring a tear out of that eye. I want to be remembered as someone who can pull emotion out of people because that's how you find the truth.

maxwell

growth

The biggest and strongest message is that whatever it is that you're called to do—do it. Every day is an opportunity for you to reach a higher level.

the biggest and strongest message is that whatever it is that you're called to do—do it. Do it regardless of whatever accolades you may receive or whatever opportunities may come your way. If it's a true conviction, then it will continue within you, whether you exercise it professionally or you do it recreationally. When you do what you are meant to do, it's not about the money. It's about the sacrifice and the dedication that you put in.

The biggest challenge for me was believing in the possibility of achieving this. That's the hardest part—allowing yourself the opportunity, giving yourself half a chance to make it. I think a lot of people tend to sabotage themselves because they're afraid of what the future holds. You have to let that go, live in the moment, live in the now, and let the future unfold for you. Even now, it's a challenge to just give myself the chance to finally make it in the way that I know I can. That's not something that has to do with the outside world. It's something more quiet and internal than that.

I think that my success was blind fate. I didn't really expect too much. A lot that happened with me initially was a result of other people having faith in what I could do. But I was just kind of happy to be making music, regardless of what the outcome was going to be. It was just, like, "Look, I make music. I'll make it after work, even if I have to do it after working at a McDonald's. I'll go home, and I'll make music."

Whatever it takes for a person to develop their craft, he or she should do it. That could be singing lessons or just singing in the shower along with every song you hear. Everyone needs to trust that inner voice that will always guide you and tell you where you need to go next.

I think every day is a big break because the process never ends. When you think of your career in terms of a big break, then you almost make yourself finite. You make the experience finite, and you limit it. Every day is an opportunity for you to reach a higher level. Or to try to. I'm still growing. It is important to be courageous enough to put yourself on the line for your art. People and artists who do that have been the biggest inspiration for me. I don't mean people who are successful and accepted on a commercial level, but people who are brave. People who reach for that courage are the ones who really make me keep trying, who make me keep working and striving.

When I was a kid, what I wanted to be when I grew up was happy. It's so hard when you're young, you're from the city, and you just don't think anything is beyond that block where you're from or that corner where you hang out. The key for me was the radio. The radio was the thing that said, "There is a way. There is a door. And it's music." I was too young to afford a record so I would listen to my parents' old records and tape my music off the radio. It wasn't so much the idea of *my* being on the radio, but just the music itself that touched me.

I was very shy as a kid so I ended up staying at home and figuring out how to make the best of the passing time. I wrote hundreds of songs before I was twenty, out of boredom, really. I had nothing to do, and that was how I had fun. Some New York clubs started to play my music and that's what led to a recording contract.

I still get nervous. It still comes. I think when you stop being nervous you should stop, period, because nervousness keeps you on your toes, keeps you humble, and keeps you knowing that you're blood, flesh, and bones. It lets you know that when you get out there and the spirit hits you, that the spirit is what drives you. I know the spirit is what drives me onstage. I don't take any credit for any of it.

there is a lesson in everything I see and hear. It's in the people who used to make music and it's in the people who are up and coming. I just try to take it all in. I'm a little hard-headed in that sometimes I think I know everything. But I'm learning to open up and listen a little bit more. I think sharing a philosophy with the people in your life is more important than sharing a profession with them. I think it's important to surround yourself with people with ideals that are similar to yours—people who have ideals that you wish to reflect.

It's important for me to try to be happy and to show people who are dear to me—people who are supportive, and people who are just a rock in my life—how much I love them, and to show them how much I appreciate them right now. I've had a tendency to never say the things that I need to say to those who have been important and instrumental in making what has happened to me happen. So, now, I try to do that. I try to let everyone around me know how much I appreciate their help and their love and guidance. I have so many people to thank.

The examples that you set—even the ones that you set unconsciously—affect and touch people. Everybody knows when they are doing wrong. It may take time, but eventually everything finds its way back to you. At the same time, I don't think you should live a lie to try to make people happy or compromise yourself in any way. I think the best way to influence other people, especially young people, is to live the truth. I try to spread the truth that there is just one love, that we all live under one power, and that there is really no separation between us. The divisions between us are an illusion.

It's important to be clear about what you think you're going to receive with the fame you get. I didn't expect to be happier because of this. I knew that this would only be a path to, or a step toward, trying to get happiness. But happiness is something that usually has nothing to do with your career—it has to do with the peace you have with yourself and with the people you love.

I tend to want everything to be perfect. But I think that I'm learning to understand the beauty in the scar. I take it one day at a time now. I try to keep in mind all the things that I went through to get to the place I am now, and I try to remember that fame is not really what it's all about. Fame is a by-product of what comes with being in this position. Music is the route and the reason why I do what I do. I can go away from fame and still be happy if I can just make the music. I've learned that the sheer joy is in the music.

tyra banks

image

It means so much to me to know that young Black women can look at me and feel beautiful because their image is somewhere it's never been before.

nothing ever just happens with me. I'm very lucky that I started modeling at a time when my look was in, but everything else is work. My parents are both very driven and my mom is supportive in a very healthy way. She has always wanted to be the best and she's shown me how to be that, too. I won't settle for second best.

The best advice my mother gave me about my career was, "Don't believe the hype!" When I was at the height of my newfound fame and everybody was telling me "You're so beautiful, and you're so this, and you're the next that," she told me, "Don't believe it. Understand that they are talking about a product, and products can go stale, they can become out of date." She taught me to separate myself from my product, to separate myself from my public image and that is what has kept me strong and level-headed. The best advice my mom gave me about men was that, for most of her life, she was *chosen* by men. So she told me, "Choose who *you* want to be with. Don't sit around waiting to be chosen. You'll be a lot happier because you'll be with the person *you* want to be with." I've never forgotten that.

i started modeling in the twelfth grade. My mom was a medical photographer so she took some pictures of me. We took the pictures to different agencies and the first five or six said no. They said that I was too ethnic-looking, or not ethnic-looking enough, or that we already have one Black girl, we don't need two Black

girls. The last one said I had a nice body frame and that I could do runway fashion shows, but that I wasn't photogenic enough for print, so I couldn't do that. So I started with fashion shows in my hometown of Los Angeles.

My mom explained to me that whatever you do, you have to study for it and prepare for it. Originally, I had planned on going to college, but two weeks before my first day, a Paris agent saw some pictures of me and my LA agency convinced me to go to Paris instead. For college, I'd had to study for the SAT. When I found out I was going to Paris, my mother said, "They're talking about you doing fashion shows, so you have to study for that, too." So I went to the fashion library and I asked them to pull out every tape that they had of Iman walking down a runway. I would sit in that library and just watch Iman over and over and over again. I would stand up and practice my walk and the librarian would laugh at me, but I didn't care because I was walking like Iman. I would also tape fashion television shows and I'd put on my mom's satin robe and her heels and sashay back and forth in the living room to perfect my walk. I used to be really known for my walk. Little did they know, I was copying Iman, but adding some flair of my own. Iman had a strong impact on me, and watching her shaped my career.

the toughest challenge of my modeling career was and still is being a Black woman. People say, "Tyra, you've made it, you've done this, you've done that." But there are tons of magazine covers I haven't done and might never do. I don't know. I'm not in control of that. But at the same time, I wouldn't trade my skin color for anything in the world.

I remember the party for my *Sports Illustrated* cover. My dad and mom flew in and it was my dad's first event, so he was really excited. When we arrived, there was this huge blowup of the cover the size of the building and it was glowing so I saw it from two blocks away! I had all of these people interviewing me about how it feels to be the first Black woman on the cover. Then Black Entertainment Television came up to me and asked the same question. But, because it was BET, I just broke down crying because I finally understood what it meant and what it stood for. It meant so much to me to know that young Black women could look at me on that cover and feel beautiful because their image was somewhere it had never been before.

acting is something that I am also passionate about. I take my craft very seriously. Like my mom says, whatever you do, you've got to study. I think I have natural acting abilities, which are being honed and perfected by studying. I diligently attend acting classes and do scene studies with all of the other actors. I also have to face the challenge of people thinking that I'm a model who can't act. But I'll show them!

I love kids. I have a strong maternal instinct. My approach to dealing with children has always been hands-on. A lot of people think, "I don't have a lot of money so I can't make a difference." But what's worth more than money is time. I have my own camp for girls called Tzone. I know a lot of people have foundations and give a lot of money, but I choose to take a different approach. Although it is self-funded, at Tzone I am there every day with the girls. I wake them up, share breakfast, lunch, and dinner with them, lead camp songs, and facilitate emotional discussions about their approaching womanhood.

My career is laced with a significant number of firsts. Although I am proud of my achievements, I am very much concerned that there are still prominent color divisions within the media. I find it extremely disheartening that in this day and age, people of color have not become a part of our nation's mainstream media view. But I have a message for the next generation of Black entertainers: Be inspired by my successes and achievements, but continue to strive for more. I've touched tip of the iceberg, but there is so much more to accomplish. Be ready for a tough and trying journey full of obstacles, challenges, and rejection. And, above all, don't let anyone tell you that you can't. I'm living proof that you can!

shaun robinson

independence

Everything that you need is already there—it just needs to be nurtured. Educate yourself and trust yourself. You can't depend on anybody but yourself.

everything that you need is already there—it just needs to be nurtured. Just educate yourself, study, become interested in learning new things, and trust yourself. You can't depend on anybody but yourself.

One time I was anchoring—it was actually later in my career, but I wish I had heard it earlier—and I was telling the producer into my microphone that I didn't know how to pronounce a certain word. It was a name from Iraq or Iran or someplace like that. And when I asked the producer, "How do you pronounce this?" he answered, "I don't know, but whatever you say, say it with confidence."

That has always stuck out in my mind. Sometimes you don't feel like you can do it at all. Sometimes you feel nervous about a big task coming up. Sometimes you feel like you might not be able to succeed or do your best in a certain area—but whatever you do, do it with confidence and you'll be all right in the end.

i'm from Detroit, Michigan. I have family in Detroit, and I have a lot of family in Georgia, too, so I have a little Southern belle about me. My mother and father were divorced when I was very young, but I remember both of them always telling me that I was very smart, that I could make it, that I could do anything that I wanted to do. Both of them instilled in me the fact that I needed to depend on *me*. I needed to become very independent. They told me to try to achieve my goals, no matter what they were, and never think anything was beyond my reach.

When I was a little girl, I wanted to be a television anchor. There was a woman who used to be on television when I was little—her name was Beverly Paine. She was the first Black woman I ever saw anchoring the news. And I remember saying, "I'd like to be just like her." She was an idol of mine. So I used to watch the news every night when I was five years old because I would see this woman on television. I would think about what it would be like to be in front of a camera. And so here I am years later—well, not that many years later.

I remember seeing *Stormy Weather* with Lena Horne and seeing the Nicholas Brothers tap dancing. I remember being in awe and thinking that this was the greatest thing since sliced bread, seeing people who looked like me on the silver screen. I also remember reading *I Know Why the Caged Bird Sings* because it was one of the first books I read that focused on a young Black girl. When I got older, I got into journalism and started taking classes in it. Even when I was in high school I took classes in journalism. I went to Spelman College in Atlanta, and majored in English and Mass Communications.

My big break came the first time that I was on the air in Detroit. I was interning, after I'd graduated from college. I called all my friends and family and said, "This is my first time on the air." They watched and everybody said, "Hey, maybe you can do this." I always knew that I would do it.

I started reporting and anchoring in Detroit, and then went on to Flint, Michigan. At the time, there were very few Black women newsanchors anywhere in the country, and there still aren't many. A news director in Flint told me that I would never make it in television, so after three and a half months at that station, I left. Then I got a job two weeks later in Milwaukee, and I started doing medical reporting, hosting a talk show, and anchoring the weekend show. From there I went to Austin, Texas. I was a reporter and anchor. Then in Miami, Florida, I anchored *The Morning Show*, which meant getting up at 3 o'clock in the morning and going to bed at 7 at night. I had no social life at all.

I've been in news my entire life. But *Access Hollywood* is my first foray into entertainment. *Access Hollywood* had heard about me and asked for a tape from my agent. They flew me out, interviewed me, and hired me.

For television anchors and reporters, there are companies that are called talent banks. Your agent—or you—might send your tape to a talent bank. A show like *Access Hollywood* calls the talent bank and says, "Show me all of your female anchors." Then they get hundreds, and hundreds, and hundreds of tapes. So out of those hundreds, and hundreds, and hundreds of tapes, they saw mine and liked it.

My career hasn't been a straight path. Often I've had to take one step back to take two steps forward. Like in Flint, Michigan, when the news director told me that I would never make it in television, and I ended up leaving the station. Part of me got really discouraged. It was like a kick in the teeth when he said it. For a moment I believed it. I thought for a moment. Just for a quick moment. And then I knew. I said to myself, "You know what? He's wrong. I know I'm going to make it." I was out of work for two weeks, but I knew that this was what I wanted to do. I knew that if it didn't happen that month, it would happen the next month, or the next. Although some jobs have come to me as pleasant surprises, I have never waited for other people to create opportunities for me. I tried to make little breaks for myself throughout my career.

At heart I'm a news journalist. I think that's in my blood. But being an entertainment journalist is certainly a lot of fun, and my background in news has definitely helped me to move forward in Hollywood. Of course, once you're out here, you become less impressed with celebrities and more impressed with normal folks who are making it on budgets that are a fraction of what celebrities have to spend. I'm impressed by people who are raising families, people like my grandmother who cleaned the houses of White people for years and would then come home and take care of us, too. She and my grandfather didn't have much money but they always had food for anybody who came by their house. Always. More and more I've become impressed by people like my grandparents, my parents, and my brother. Those are the people who are the real stars.

In Hollywood, everything fades after a while. That's why my family and my friends are my top priority. When you've really found some people who are well grounded, down-to-earth, and people who genuinely love you—not because you're on television, not because you can put them in touch with a very famous person, but because they love you for *you*—you have to make time to be with those people. They really give you the nourishment you need to continue every day.

If you are interested in journalism, read a lot. Read newspapers, learn new words, study. Talk to interesting people. Try to know a little bit about a lot of different things. The most important thing is to have confidence. I think that African-American children need to learn from the time they are very little that we come from a very strong people. Our race has built this country, and we have a right to be here. Don't for a minute think that your skin is too dark, your nose is too wide, that because you look like this that you're not good enough. We have to make our children aware that we are beautiful—we are a beautiful people. Just believe that you are as special as anyone else out there. That is the bottom line. Believe in yourself, and believe in what you want to become. Just believe.

leon robinson

individuality

*I've never wanted to be the most successful. I wanted to be me, and I
wanted to do the things that are uniquely me. As long as I'm true to
myself, I feel no threat from anyone else.*

i was never part of the crowd. I was always doing something different. I've been
influenced most by my parents and how they allowed me to be an individual—to
be different. My parents didn't always take my being different well, but in the end
they always allowed me to be myself. That's enabled me to be myself in my acting and in everything I do.

Your individuality is what sets you apart from other people. As long as I'm true
to myself, I feel no threat from anyone else. We need more people to be individuals and have other people follow their trends, as opposed to following *the* trend.

As far as my projects are concerned, I approach each one in a very individual
way. I'm not as concerned with showing myself (we have the media for that) as I
am with showing the essence of the character I'm portraying.

I'm not trying to get into the game just because I see other people doing it. I'm
not very competitive with my fellow actors. I know a lot of people are, and I think
that's a good driving force for some people, but that's not what motivates me.
Anyone else's success to me is great, especially if they are African-American. I
think it's great. I've never wanted to be the most successful. I wanted to be me. I
wanted to do the things that are uniquely me.

Acting wasn't something I always wanted to do. Acting kind of found me. The
first thing I ever thought I wanted to be was a priest. That's because I went to
Catholic schools, and at mass, everyone always sat quietly, and the only one talk-

ing was the priest. I thought, *Well, I could do that!* Then I found out that priests couldn't be with women, and I wasn't feeling that. I realized that my interest in being a priest was based on my need to be up there in front of people.

I had never even thought of acting until I saw my sister's high-school stage production. We used to have a variety show at my school, and I wanted to do something like my sister's show. I was in the eighth grade. A friend and I choreographed all the numbers and cast everyone, and it was a big success. That was my first taste of being onstage.

Unfortunately, I was at an all-boys prep academy that didn't have a drama department so I just excelled in athletics. I became all-city as a basketball player and had a very normal life. I think that playing sports was good preparation for what I'm doing now. It taught me how to be the focal point of attention and to deal with pressure that comes with that.

I was in college at Loyola Marymount in Los Angeles when one day a graduate film student chased me down campus to be in his movie. And I was like, "Why me? There are all those people studying theater arts, why don't you get one of them, I'm sure they would love to be in your film?" And he said, "It's just the way you look. I just see you in movies." So I acted in his movie.

I had an experience that we all have at some point. You can be sitting talking to someone, whether it's a man, a woman, or a child, for an hour when suddenly you get the feeling that you've known this person for so much longer than just that little time you have spent with them. That's the way I felt the first time I was on a movie set. I felt as though I was at home. I was in California at the time, and I came back to New York and studied acting and started making movies and now I'm being interviewed by Matthew Jordan Smith. (I guess I've made it!)

Race is definitely an issue. Any person of color who enters this business has to know that you have that working against you right up front. You know that going in, so just go after what you need to go after and get it. If you're not prepared for that issue, go into something else where your chances are better. The toughest challenge is always the same—the persistence, the patience, the dealing with rejection. I'm in a business where even if people say no to you nine out of the ten times, that one yes means you are very successful. To be successful is to do the things that are important to you regardless of what other people think, say, or do. I'm always striving to do that.

As far as women, what happens with a lot of male actors is that when things start happening, you go from sweating girls to girls sweating you. Some people don't handle it really well, and you see some guys who have horrible reputations even though they're not bad people at all. It's just because they don't know how to deal with success yet.

I was lucky. I grew up in a family where I was the only male in my generation. I grew up around women so I learned to love and respect them before my hormones kicked in. I just like women and I think they sense that and so I have a lot of female friends. As I became more well known, attention from women isn't something I had a hard time dealing with because I was always cool with them. The only drama in my life is on screen.

One thing I was always told is that first impressions mean a lot, so don't go in before you are ready because people always remember the first time—whether it's in a meeting, or at an audition, or in a casual encounter. That first impression really lasts in people's heads, so you should be ready for it.

An entertainment attorney once told me, "Every time you make a film, you make a documentation of your career." So every time people look back at the films you've done, and they make a note of it, it's almost like your age or when you graduated from high school. This is the point where you were here. I've incorporated that knowledge into my career decisions. You have to be able to go to sleep every night feeling good about yourself. That's why it's important to me that I do projects that have some integrity. I always try to stay focused on why I'm here. The reason I act is to tell stories. I want to make movies that affect people. I want to touch them. I want to move them.

I want to be good at whatever I am. I've always wanted to be a really good friend. I've always wanted to be a really good boyfriend. I've always wanted to be a great husband and a great father. I want to do my best at whatever I try to do, and I feel acting is what I'm supposed to be doing, and that's why I'm giving it everything I've got.

kenny lattimore

I didn't get into this for the money. I got into this for the music, for the feeling it gives me and for the inspiration that it gives others.

for all of us, the challenges are finding yourself and staying true to who you are. When I talk about "finding yourself," I don't mean it in a mysterious way. I just mean being in touch with your purpose and knowing how you plan on giving back. I was always taught to put the music first. That means focusing on the message and recognizing that, for me, music is a tool, a communicative vehicle for me to express myself and give back to the world. I didn't get into this for the money. I got into this for the music, for the feeling it gives me, and for the inspiration that it gives others. Inspiration brings out the best in people. It enlightens us, expands our vision, creates new goals, and makes us believe that we can achieve them.

I have always been inspired by other artists. I try not to just incorporate stylistic elements, but to convey to the listener the same feelings those artists generated in me. Inspiration is about experiencing those emotions, making them your own, and sharing them with others.

My family had always affirmed my musical abilities, but the first time I started to take them seriously was when I was about ten. My next-door neighbor, Andrea, had invited a bunch of girls over to her house one day. All of a sudden, there was a knock on the door. It was Andrea, who asked, "Kenneth, can you come over here and sing us a song?" She had told her friends, "Kenneth can really sing and I just want you all to hear this because you won't believe how talented he is." So I sang a little piece of a song—I can't even remember what the song was—and all the girls started screaming. And I thought, *Oh! There's some power to this!* I realized at that moment that I had touched their lives in some way. It made me understand the power of music. I found it very fulfilling, and it gave me the courage to keep going.

In many ways, music has always been a part of my life—my parents sang, my grandmother played piano, and there was always music in the house. My mother was a college counselor in Pennsylvania, so she would take me to shows that featured the artists I really admired. I was so excited by their energy, by the way they inspired an audience. I was so caught up in it. But more than that, I felt I could do it.

After that, my friend Marcus and I would lock ourselves away in our rooms, make instruments from brooms and cardboard boxes, and try to create that same excitement. One day, my mother happened to overhear me and thought, *Okay, my son sings well. Maybe he'll be interested in taking some vocal classes and training his voice.* My cousin, Marilyn, taught voice professionally and she took me under her wing. I started singing standards and by high school, I was performing in a choir singing chamber music and classical pieces in about nine different languages. My high school had one of the best music programs in the nation. We competed and won international competitions. That fed my confidence, and gave me my first taste of being a performer. It also built up my nerve to move forward professionally, to try to be like the people who had awakened my own artistic sensibility.

My mom started managing me when I was fourteen. Initially, I performed locally with bands in clubs. My mom shielded me from the things she felt could be detrimental and helped expose me to the business side of my career. In fact, my entire family got involved and fully supported me. My sister is a gospel singer and she helped me write a song for a band I was in called Maniquin. She taught me how to loosen up and put the human experience into my writing. The result was the first song we ever recorded for a major label, "Now and Then."

One of the hardest things to deal with at the start of my professional career was identifying who I really was as a person and bringing that to my music. Although I grew up singing in parish choirs, it wasn't until I was a teenager that my mom got me more involved in the church and gospel music. I knew I didn't want to sing gospel music exclusively, but I understand why gospel is often referred to as "inspirational music" because it inspired me. I started writing my own songs because I wanted to sing about the human experience in its purest form. We all share the same experiences, and that's what I like to write about.

The first time I really felt I had turned the corner as a writer and a performer was when I returned home to Washington, DC, to do a free concert for a radio station. Thousands of people were waiting. When I came out, they were screaming and singing along to my songs. For the first time, I felt different. I had grown from being the boy in the basement writing those songs to the man onstage singing those songs and receiving the admiration of the people of my city.

My mother always said, "To whom much is given, much is required." I try to use my talent to convey a message that's going to touch people's lives in a positive way, just as my role models did for me. I'm willing to take the responsibility for reaching out and pulling somebody along with me. We all need to reach out to children, to personally interact with them, to speak to them, to teach them, to hug them and love them.

My biggest challenge today is staying true to myself, being in touch with what I feel my purpose is and having a plan of how to achieve my goals. I'm in touch with who I am as a singer and as a man in terms of my music, my family, and my purpose in life. I feel peaceful and settled. I am inspired by the possibilities for the future, and I feel like there are no limits or boundaries to what I can accomplish.

halle berry

integrity

It feels really good to have my dignity and hold my head high. I've been given a gift. I cannot drop the ball. I have to take what's been given to me and make a difference.

anybody, Black or White, who reaches any level of success has a responsibility to be a leader. They have to pay their debt to humanity because they've been given a gift. Today, there's a whole generation of young people that is mimicking, and watching, and aspiring to do what celebrities do. I am really just horrified when I see people misuse that power and not take it seriously. I feel the responsibility, too. I've been given a gift. I'm blessed, and I cannot drop the ball. I have to take what's been given to me and make a difference. I have the desire to really do that.

I think my responsibility—as a Black woman and an actress—is to take us places we haven't been, to cross color lines, and to try to lead our work in a direction where all people can enjoy it and relate to it. That is the challenge that I think is facing me right now, and I'm trying to figure out how to meet it. Do I do that in front of the camera, behind the camera? How do I begin to make that shift for us as a people? Each new year, I realize how I'm better, smarter, and wiser. I can act on my own free will and make a better contribution because I know more. That's the best part of being a grownup.

My friend and fifth-grade teacher, Yvonne Sims, gave me the best advice I ever received. She told me to remain true to myself and to not compromise my integrity, my values, or my morals for this industry. Because it's not worth it. And I've never yet felt that I've compromised myself for a job, or in any project that I've ever done. It feels really good to have my dignity and still hold my head high.

Yvonne was the only Black teacher at my grade school in Ohio, where I was one of only five Black students. She helped me understand being Black and helped me find pride in it, even though I was in a sea of white faces and had so many things that made me question who I was. Despite those challenges, my childhood was wonderful. My mother worked very hard, and it was only as an adult that I realized the sacrifices she made, the things she went without so that we could have. My mother is White, but she made it very clear early on that I was Black and that I would have to deal with racism. She helped me embrace who I was and did her best to educate me about my history, my heritage, and my culture. Although she never suffered the kind of racism we would eventually know, she felt it because she had two Black children in the 60s.

In high school, I was an overachiever. I always felt like I had to prove that I was as good as my White peers. Going to school was like a job. I was in every club, on every board, president of this and that. I was a cheerleader, in drama club, editing the newspaper. I did everything. I was really exhausted during those years trying to prove, prove, prove. I thought that, by the end of high school, I had been accepted. But when the school voted me prom queen, the principal accused me of stuffing the ballot box because he couldn't believe that a Black girl could win their symbol of beauty. They tried to make me share it with the girl who had the next-highest number of votes. She was White, blue-eyed, with blond hair. We decided to toss a coin, because neither one of us wanted to be co-nothing. So we tossed a coin, and I won anyway.

That's when I realized that no matter how hard I work, no matter how smart I am, no matter how beautiful I think I am, I'm still going to be Black in America. And people are still going to try to deny me what's rightfully mine. That was a rude awakening. But it served me well, because in that moment I got it. I completely got it.

In this business, it's important to keep people around you who love and care about you, who are grounded and centered, and who will keep you level-headed in the midst of an industry that can be very heady and superficial. On a professional level, I try to surround myself with the best people who are as passionate as I am about whatever it is I'm trying to do. I rely on them to help me because I realize that I cannot do it all by myself.

The entertainment industry is not really very glamorous at all. Rejection is not glamorous, and I've had to deal with rejection. Not only personally, like in romantic love situations, but professionally all the time. It's glamorous on about ten nights of the year, when you get to dress up and go to award shows. The glamor you see on those nights is all the glamor there is. The rest is hard work, long hours, doing whatever you need to do to keep your instrument in shape. The industry is far too overrated for being glamorous.

I'm excited for Black people, for where we're going, and for the kinds of changes that are being made. While we are still being bombarded by a lot of negative images, I'm happy there are many more positive images being presented, and so many positive people emerging and becoming leaders, and taking their jobs as leaders very seriously.

I never really know if I'm on top. But I know that I am very passionate about what I'm doing, and I'm convinced that this is what I'm here to do. And that sort of fuels my passion. I now know that I can do it, and that's what keeps me going. That's what inspires me today. Now I know that whatever I dream, I can make happen. When it will happen is not the point. As long as I continue to try and push that ball forward, it will eventually happen. It will happen in God's time.

If I had to start my life over again, I wouldn't do anything differently. Not one single thing. I'd cry every tear. For me, success means freedom. It means the ability to invite change. It means history. It means making history. And that's what I'm here to do.

gregory hines

joy

It's a difficult choice to decide that one wants to be an artist, but it is a wonderful choice. I feel so happy. I feel that tap dancing is in very good feet.

i practice every day. I dance every day. And I love it. I used to dance only when I was working when I was a young man. But then as I got older, I noticed that if I didn't dance for a month, when I put my shoes back on, it wasn't as easy. I worked with Mikhail Baryshnikov, and he took a barre class every day. Even if he stayed out late the night before, he would still show up at ballet studio in the morning to take a class. So I thought, *Well, that's a good idea. I should dance every day.* So now I do it, and I get even more pleasure from tap dancing now than I did when I was younger. Whenever I get in an elevator and there's no one there, I will usually dance. There's just something about an elevator. They always have a little boom sound to them, so it sounds really nice. I have danced up a storm in an elevator between the tenth floor and the seventh floor. When the doors open, people wonder if there was a problem because of the noise. Then when they see me, they say, "Oh. Don't stop!" I just love to dance in elevators.

I love the energy that passes back and forth between artists and audiences. I love the feeling of going out there, and just giving people whatever gift I have to give. It is so much fun to be an artist in this culture. It's a very difficult choice to decide that one wants to be an artist, but it is a wonderful choice and a very satisfying one.

I always wanted to be a dancer. When I was three years old, somebody came around offering free tap lessons, and my parents gave me and my brother

Maurice those lessons. Back in the mid- to late-40s, when I was born, the scope of what a Black person could achieve was limited so I think my parents thought, one day, that this might be something that could help us earn a living. Their dream worked because we enjoyed it. We always loved dancing for people.

Racism was something that one couldn't avoid. We had to deal with segregation as performers and in everyday life. I remember as a kid visiting Florida and seeing the "White" and "Colored" water fountains and thinking, *I don't want colored water. I want the regular water.* Even in my young mind, I knew that behind those two fountains, the pipes were coming from the same place.

In addition to my parents, the people I looked up to were tap dancers—people like the Nicholas Brothers and the Step Brothers, and Honi Coles and Chooly Atkins and Sandman Sims and Bunny Briggs and Buster Brown—they were all my heroes. They taught me about professionalism and consistency. No matter what was wrong with them, no matter what was going on in their personal lives, they could put that aside and be professional and consistent and perform for an audience that had paid to see them. They never let anything prevent them from going on and doing a good show. I was very fortunate to have that example at a very young age.

Sammy Davis, Jr. influenced me the most. The first time I saw him was at the Apollo Theater in 1956. By the time I was ten, I was a pretty decent tap dancer, but that's all I could do. He came out onstage and he sang, he played instruments, he did impersonations, and he twirled cowboy pistols. And in addition to all that, he tap-danced, which was the only thing I could do. I just couldn't believe he could do all those other things, so from that point on I just wanted to be Sammy Davis. He gave me the best advice I ever received. He encouraged me to be versatile. He felt that there weren't a lot of opportunities for Black performers so if I was versatile— if I could sing in addition to dance, if I could act, if I could be funny—it would increase my opportunities for employment. Whenever I get around young people who want to be professional dancers, I always encourage them to take some acting classes, take some singing classes. If they audition for a show that's 95 percent dance, but they have to sing thirty-two bars of a song in the second act, I remind them that if they can't sing, they won't get the part. That advice stuck with me and I have tried to pass it on to as many people as I could.

For anybody who wants to get into tap, the most important thing at first is to learn the basics and study with a lot of different teachers because each teacher has something unique to share. After you learn the basics, it's important to get out there and try to get a job, to audition. Getting that first job is the toughest challenge for any artist. Even though the pay is meager in the beginning, it's important because it gives you the pride of getting paid for what you're doing. You're getting a sense of dancing as an occupation. A job also gives you the opportunity to be around professionals who can continue to teach you.

I'm very impressed with young people today. I know that in our culture, the negative sells. But most young people today are really great. They are really on top of it. They have amazing aspirations and abilities. It's just, every now and then, the few that don't have it together are the ones that get the attention, but we have to remember to pay just as much, if not more, attention to all of the really wonderful young people in our communities. Young people make me excited about the future and what they're going to bring to it.

I feel so happy. I feel that tap dancing is in very good feet, shall we say, as opposed to in very good hands. It's in very good feet. Because we have a real champion in Savion Glover. We have somebody who can actually take it and revolutionize it, which he already has. And so from this pool of young dancers, I'll be able to do some choreography that up until now I haven't been able to do. So you know, I'm just tickled. I'm tickled.

I am also very lucky because I picked the right parents. I grew up in a loving, nurturing family where I got as much love as I could handle. So when I work, I feel like I have more to thank than just my own skills. I feel like I have all these role models, and my family and the support of everybody to keep pushing. My success feels like a victory for everybody.

iman

legacy

*I don't care about fame. I care about the longevity of my career. I care
about the impact of my career. Legacy is the most important thing.*

i don't care about fame. I care about the longevity of my career. I care about the
impact of my career. I care about my legacy. I want the impact. I want the author-
ity. I want people, when they think of this business, to think that I am part of that
destiny, to think that I am not one of the models of my time but that I am one of
the models of *all* time. Legacy is the most important thing to me.

Everything happens for a reason and at the right time. Regardless of what anybody says, if you really believe in yourself, you can succeed. There are certain
things that you cannot change, but one of the things you can change is your mind.
You have to be optimistic. If you're going after what you want, and you're clear
about what you want, there is nobody in the world who can stop you. I know that
I would never have been successful in this country if there were not Black models
before me who already had worked very to hard to get the door open. They
cracked the door open, and I just kicked it down.

I was born in Somalia, in East Africa. My father was an ambassador, but we
went into exile when a military regime came to power. I was born at the height of
Somali independence. As a country, we thought that there was nothing that we
couldn't achieve. That's what influenced me as a person: the beauty of Somalia
and of my people, their pride. I have never been considered beautiful in my country. In my country, the women are extremely beautiful, so those with my beauty
are a dime a dozen. I didn't even have a date for the prom. My father had to pay
one of my cousins to take me. I was never told I was beautiful until I became a

model. All the same, one never forgets having to pay someone to take them to the prom! Beauty has never been the most important thing to me. I have never let my looks define me.

I was in Kenya, studying political science at the University of Nairobi, when a man stopped me in the street and asked if I had ever been photographed. I was so insulted. I thought it was typical of a White man to think that because I'm African I've never seen a camera. I told him that of course I had been photographed by my parents. He asked if I'd ever been photographed professionally, and all I could think of was dirty magazines! I said, "I'm not that kind of a girl." But he kept talking. It turned out that he was Peter Beard, a professional photographer. I agreed to let him take my picture, with a chaperone present, in exchange for school tuition.

Peter Beard had a photo exhibition in New York, and my photograph was on the cover of the invitation. That is how Wilhelmina of Wilhelmina Model Agency came to know of me and invited me to America. I came here in October 1975. I didn't know a soul here. I was eighteen. I had never left home alone, never worn makeup, never worn heels, and never seen a fashion magazine. I just came for the ride. My first job was for American *Vogue,* which I did on my fourth day in New York. It was like learning on the job at the speed of light. I was thrown into the eye of the hurricane.

The opportunities I had were created by earlier Black models, and I continued the tradition they started. I was the first person of color to get a major cosmetics contract, and I ultimately had the most advertisement campaigns for a Black girl in this country, ever. Black models get a lot of editorial and runway work, but we are often denied advertising campaigns, which is where most of the money is for models. It's a double standard. I hope I was able to challenge that and create more opportunities for Black women. That is my legacy.

When I became successful, I also tried to employ Black makeup artists and hairdressers because a lot of very talented people weren't being hired because of racism. I think that is one responsibility that comes with making it. You have to help people. You have to bring people with you. Bethann Hardison is my agent and my best friend. Together, we created the Black Girls Coalition to fight racism in our industry and to help promote Black talent. In the old 60s revolutionary way, we wanted to highlight Black representation and influence major corporations to change their way of working. We withdrew from the spotlight for a while, but now the Black Girls Coalition is coming back stronger than ever!

I started my cosmetics line because I realized that there was a void in the market. White women have twenty lines in the market for them, and I wanted to give women of color more options. My line was not created just for African-American women, but for all women of color: Asian, Hispanic, and Native American. When we come together, people of color in America are the majority. Sheer population growth has changed the concept of what a woman of color is. I wanted to celebrate that.

I've always felt that to whom much is given, much is expected. I come from a country that believes a life of service is much more important than a life of self, and that's how I was raised. I realize I have influence because I was the first model of my caliber to come out of Africa so I have become a very politically active person. I've always voiced my concerns about the Third World, and specifically about Africa. I've always found that in politics, you have more influence on the outside than when you are on the inside. When you're on the outside, you don't have to play by their rules. You can ruffle feathers, speak your mind, and voice your point of view. I'm celebrated by Africans, but not because of my beauty. They see beyond that. I'm still very connected to Africa, and that's what they see. That I am very connected to Somalia, to humanitarian issues, and to children throughout the world.

My biggest worry about many children today is that they only see the success, and they don't see the process of how to get that success. They never hear how people got there, the sacrifices that people have to make, the time that's spent in doing the actual work. Everything is made out to be an overnight success. The truth is that people have worked for ten or fifteen years to get to where they are. They have honed their craft. A lot of kids want people to "show them the money." Everybody wants to be a CEO, but nobody wants to do the work. My biggest worry for young people is that many of them don't have a work ethic. My advice to them would be to get one, to understand the process of working, and to realize that it's not always about the money. You have to have your passions. You have to know what you want to do in your life. Get the money out of the way and focus on the passion that you have for that work. If you're willing to work hard twenty-four hours a day, seven days a week, it will pay off. The more you give, the more you will get.

The most important thing in my life is to live as honestly as I can. At the end of the day I want to be remembered as African, dignified, and as a woman who challenged the beauty system.

monica

mothers and mentors

*A lot of times, we don't want to take responsibility for our actions. We
want to run to the politicians, and we want to run to the media, and
we say they need to clean things up. I think if we clean up some of our
households first, we could alleviate a lot of the painful things that our
children experience. Because that's what my mother did.*

a lot of people say their mother had the biggest impact on their lives, but I can
honestly say I mean it. She was a single mother. When my father was not doing the
things he should have been doing, instead of bad-mouthing him, she would always try to help me understand what happened. That helped me as an adult because I didn't suffer like a lot of people I've met who feel that things happened in
their childhood because of them. She worked all of her life to protect me from that.

Sometimes, we don't want to take responsibility for our actions. We want to run
to the politicians, and we want to run to the media, and we say they need to clean
things up. I think if we clean up some of our households first, we could alleviate a lot
of the painful things that our children experience because that's what my mother did.

I can tell her anything. We do everything together. I try to learn from her. Sometimes when I'm really confused, I'll watch her. I let her be my guide. She is my first
love. I'd give my life to make sure that my family's life is right. After all my mother
has endured, I feel that she is very deserving. The fact that she doesn't ever ask
makes me want to do twice as much.

I started singing in church. We had a family choir made up of about fifteen of
us. At nine years old, I sang "The Greatest Love of All" at a pageant we had, and
it just continued from there. I started doing these talent shows around the city. I

was this little girl with the ponytail who always sang this same song, and people started to remember me and talk about me. One day Kevin Wells was in a barbershop where people were discussing me. He got some information on me from a friend of ours. He went on to introduce me to Dallas Austin.

Many people are curious about how I started calling him Daddy, but I never remember calling him Dallas. I was eleven when he started really spending time with me. We were more like a family than a company. He made sure that I enjoyed my life as a child because at that time, he didn't have any children of his own. He would do things that my mother would have done for me. He felt that it was really important that I knew I was loved because he didn't want me to be insecure and searching for love like a lot of people in this industry. He made me a priority. He made me wait several years to release my album because he was very adamant about me knowing who I was before I allowed media and the industry to be a part of my life. He was right because I don't know if I was mentally prepared at eleven, twelve, or thirteen. At fourteen—surprisingly enough because that's still a young age—I was really mentally ready.

My cousin, Melinda Dancil, is my manager. She was in college when she started putting me in talent shows, and she was spending all her school money making sure that I had new outfits to perform in. She gave up a lot because she knew what was coming for me. She eventually gave up a good job to manage me. Once she did that, I gave my all to her. When it came time to negotiate my contract, she read all sorts of books that gave us knowledge a record company would never have wanted us to have. Instead of being puppets on a string, we came to the table, like, "This is what we want." We were confident at all times. When we didn't know something, we might have to run, run, run to those books. But we didn't let them see that. Because of her, I came out in a much, much better position than a lot of people. I've never had those terrible deals that you hear about because Melinda gave her life to make sure that I didn't.

Another person who has been a very good friend to me is Whitney Houston. When I first met her, she immediately seemed like the sister I'd never had. The best advice she ever gave me was not about my career; it was about how to maintain my personal life with my career. She explained to me that love will come in all forms, but love that was real would withstand the test of time. She told me not to allow myself to become a victim of losing my life to entertainment. Whitney still gives me advice.

When we first heard one of my songs on the radio, we just went crazy. The song was, "Just One of Them Days," and I think we spent the whole song going from cell phone to cell phone calling each other. I still get excited every time I hear my music being played on the radio. Each new song has its own meaning so I just get excited all over again every time I hear one.

I was very afraid in the beginning, afraid of something I did not understand. It wasn't that I didn't have confidence in my talent. I just didn't know if people were ready to accept everything that I was. I was not groomed to do this. I would say what I felt and be shunned because other young people that were out at that time constantly skated around issues. But because of where I grew up, I saw so many things that concerned me, like teen pregnancy, violence, and drug abuse. I felt I was blessed with the opportunity to be able to speak, to let other young people know that there are people who love them and are there for them because that's what I saw in a lot of people as I was growing up—a lack of love.

For the first two years of my career, people would say, "It was almost like she's not really fourteen." Or "She's too grown." But I stayed strong and true to what I believe. And I was just right!

I think the best way to influence people is to speak our minds clearly. Some people really appreciated my honesty. Other people really liked it that I was hungry. I was a raw talent. I wasn't cut and shaped and molded and formed to what people wanted and expected at that time. I never focused on fame. Instead, I focused on me. I kept saying, "Well, yeah, at this point, I've had four number-one songs, and I've sold however many records, but you know what? There's something else I want to do." I constantly put more things in my head that I want to achieve. Then, I sit down and start working.

Dedication and determination are the only two things you need to be successful. People have their own myths about what it takes. People say, "Well, give me some press shots or bring me demos," but we are not all in a position where we can afford to do that. What you really need is complete dedication to your craft. I remember sneaking into shows and singing backstage for people. If that's what it takes, then that's what you do. I didn't ever have demos or press shots and all the other things that we think it takes to make it. I never had those things so I hope that people around me—people who have been in my position, or people who are from a background like mine—know that they can accomplish whatever they want. I hope they get that from me.

When I set my mind to something, I do it. I hope that other people feel that if I did it, they can do it, too.

debbie allen

movement

You try to anticipate, but then you just have to flow with that river,
honey. Just make sure you don't drown on the way.

in the dance world, we are born of criticism. We are made by it. So criticism is a part of learning. Criticism may not always feel good, but it certainly will point you to where you might want to go or not go. I have a real thick skin for criticism because in the dance world, that's what happens to us. That and also being critical of yourself and continuing to try new things. You have to keep trying things and exploring. My mom always said, "It's not good enough to be really great at what you do. You have to understand *why* you are great, why you are doing it, and you have to keep going."

My mama, Vivian Ayres Allen, is a Renaissance woman. She's an artist, a writer, a painter, and a classical pianist. She's one of the most beautiful women ever to grace the earth. She does everything. In learning to do all the things she was doing, my sister, Phylicia Rashad, and I developed our own identities as artists. We were all destined to be in the arts, but Phylicia was more into music and singing, and I was into dancing. I think I was born dancing.

Mama kept me on the straight and narrow path. There were a few times that I could have stopped, but my mother kept me going forward. It wasn't that I wanted to actually quit dancing. But I was discouraged because, when I was growing up, Black children were not allowed to do anything. You couldn't go downtown, you couldn't go to the amusement park, and you couldn't go to ballet class. I found lessons in spite of that, but, at times, I felt very discouraged as a Black girl and later as a Black woman. There was no place for me. But I was definitely talented, and

Mama kept me in it. She made me feel responsible for my own successes or failures and didn't allow me to lay off on anything. She kept me focused. Then I saw Alvin Ailey's company, and I knew I could do it. Child, I saw those sisters with those butts and those heels and I said, "Oh, yes, honey, throw out those toe shoes. Let me wade in the water. I'm ready to wade in the water."

Dance led me to all of these different wonderful things that I do now. My friend Suzanne de Passe calls me Dusty because she says I'm like Dust. I'm everywhere. I do a lot of things. But I call her Windy because I say that if I'm everywhere, she's the wind blowing me. She's right there with me.

The hardest challenge for me in moving from dance into directing and producing was being a woman. It was tough getting the boys to chill out and recognize that a woman—5'2" little wide-butt woman—might know a lot more than they think. That wasn't every man, but there were some challenges that were definitely there because I was a woman. But I've never let that stop me.

Even when I'm working, I'm always training and studying. I'm always learning something new, trying something new. I was paying a lot of attention so by the time I went through all the paces from dancing on Broadway, to choreographing, directing, and producing for television, I was ready to produce the movie, *Amistad.* That was the culmination of everything that I had done up until then. I had to work on that production as the mother, the choreographer, the head researcher. I had to be a scholar, and I had to be a strong producer, to support my director, Steven Spielberg, who is just a genius. Sometimes, genius is not so easy to work with because you can't always predict where it is going to go. So you try to anticipate, but then you just have to flow with that river, honey. Just make sure you don't drown on the way.

It's vital to learn from those you admire and are inspired by. If you want to be a great pianist, you have to have a great teacher. If you want to be a writer, you just read every great book you can get your hands on and try to get a sense of how the language has been used. It's not possible to reach that goal by yourself. You need guidance—we all do—and direction along the way. It's a must. Growing up, I would say that books had a greater influence on me than almost anything else, especially photographs of dancers. Those books helped me envision a future for myself as a dancer.

Success is fleeting. Success is that project, that period, that time. It is not an end in itself. It is a road that does not end. So if you're seeking success, know that you're in for a long ride because success is not just one accomplishment. Something great could happen, and it's fantastic. But then tomorrow, you've got to start over. The challenge is facing the reality of that cycle.

If I could start all over again, I probably might have done a couple of things a little differently, made a couple of choices that I didn't make and said yes to some things that I said no to. But I'm happy with myself and my life experiences. I've had a glorious life when it comes to connecting the dots. I kind of like the picture that's there right now.

I'm still dreaming. Being a dreamer is part of who I am. I'm still that five-year-old kid back in Houston, Texas, looking at that wide open sky and staring at all those stars and figuring out where I'm going to land in the universe next.

holly robinson-peete

Being a successful actress requires thick skin, a lot of ambition,
and a good hair stylist.

you're not guaranteed anything in this business. You get this one little shot. When you get your first shot, whatever you do with it basically sets up what's going to happen in the future. You're not even guaranteed the first shot so you're certainly not guaranteed a second shot. So if you are fortunate enough to get your shot, you've got to take it, you've got to roll with it. You've got to expand it. I was fortunate that I took my shot and made the best of it. I think that's why I've been able to sustain a consistent career in television to this point. My mom, Delores Robinson, is a manager who has carved out an amazing business in a White-male-dominated industry. She has been an unbelievable inspiration.

Before I became famous, I had a little preview of fame, because I had a chance to watch my mother manage careers of actors who came and went. I got a good chance to watch these actors make mistakes before *I* had to make them. It's like your parents—when they make mistakes in life they want you to learn from them. But you don't have to go through the drama, the pain of making mistakes and ruining your own career.

So when I got my chance, I was able to step up to the plate and say, "Okay, this is my shot." I knew proper etiquette. I knew how to treat people, and I knew how to deal with the public. I was very fortunate in that way because not everybody gets that opportunity. They get it thrust upon them, and they're not ready. There are a lot of people who are not ready for success. I really think you're either prepared to deal with it or you're not. But one of the ways to become prepared is to watch and learn from the people around you, and to work hard to make the right decisions and the right impression.

I grew up half in Philadelphia and half in California. My father was the original Gordon on *Sesame Street*. It had a profound effect on me in the same way that it's influenced most children. It was an educational program that celebrates the inner city and gives kids across the country the opportunity to see people who look different from them. Sometimes it was confusing because my parents had separated, and I would turn on the TV and think, *Well, what's Daddy doing there when he's supposed to be here?* But it was still wonderful. I got to go to parties with Oscar and Big Bird, Ernie and Bert. That's not a bad deal for a five-year-old. As an actress, I got my feet wet on *Sesame Street* because I got to be on the show a couple times. Even then I really liked being in front of the camera.

What really made me want to be in show business was seeing the Broadway play *Purlie*. I was about seven, and I saw Melba Moore up there singing *Purlie*, and I said, "Okay, this is what I want to do!"

Most of the actors I went to high school with in Malibu, California, did not go to college. They went right into movies and some are very famous. I guess that worked for them, but my father threatened me within an inch of my life so I *had* to go to school. He refused to support my being in show business until he knew I had gotten my bachelor's degree. I'm glad he forced me to go because I now know how valuable an education is.

My big break really came after I graduated from Sarah Lawrence College, and I got a role on *21 Jumpstreet*. They liked my ability to find the character and make her my own, to make her really likable. That was something I learned by example from watching my mother in the business and watching other actors. I paid attention so when I got my shot I was really ready. Ever since I first started on *21 Jumpstreet* in 1987 I have consistently been on television. I'm still working, and I am really blessed in that respect.

Being a successful actress requires thick skin, a lot of ambition, and a good hair stylist. You need all those things. I know some women who can do their own makeup, but hair is another story. You have got to have that hair working, you know what I'm saying?

On a serious note, it's very important to be able to know that a lot of things that happen are not personally about you. The hardest thing is separating what's personal from what's just business, especially when you confront the rejection part of the industry. At the same time, it's important to make sure that you are not one of the people who makes this business difficult or painful for someone else.

One of the most important things I've learned is that you better be nice to people who you see on the way up because you will definitely see those same people on the way down. It's the oldest cliché in the world, but there is nothing more true. Be nice to the people you see on the way up because they're going to remember, and when times are hard, they will help you.

For example, I have a friend who is now a very successful studio executive but used to be an actor. He always told me that you have got to be a people person, you have got to be respectful to people. When he was an actor, he had a small part on a major television show in the 70s. The lead actor on the show was very nasty to him. Years later, when that actor needed a career boost, he approached this executive to try to pitch a show and get back on track. But the exec remembered all too well how rude the former star was to him some fourteen years before. It had really hurt him so the executive said to the actor, "Do you remember me?" and the actor said. "Of course. You're so and so, you're a big executive." But the executive said, "No, no, no, I was on episode 555 on March 1, 1972." If the former star had been nice to him, when he came to him later in life, the exec would have helped him. I always remember that story because I know that those are the kinds of things that you have to deal with down the road. That taught me a lesson that I've never forgotten.

I have also realized that as Black people, we're starved for images of ourselves. Unfortunately, because of that, we tend to go to some movies that are not particularly good just to see other Black people on the screen. Doing that limits the kinds of projects that are being produced and the quality of those projects. We've got to make it a priority to support our best work, to become stronger and more competitive. We have to force the industry to take us seriously as people who spend a lot of money on entertainment and who deserve to see excellent projects.

I've had a very successful career, but my main priority is my family. Some may say that I could have a better career, that it could be bigger, but I don't have those aspirations. My aspirations center around being happy and making sure my kids and my husband are happy—having everyone taken care of. I don't need all the excesses. I'm just so happy with what I have.

ray allen

overtime

When everybody else is relaxing and trying to enjoy themselves, I still work. You've got to work when everybody else is playing. You've got to find fuel for your fire every day.

i always said, "I want to be the best, and I want to be extra special, and I want people to look at me, like, 'He's amazing!'" But that comes through doing extra. You have to do the extra work that everybody else isn't doing. Not everybody knows that.

I learned that from one of my coaches. He told me, "If you want to have a long career in professional basketball, you've got to do extra. If you want to be some-thing special, you've got to stop doing things that hold you back. If you want to be special, you can't do what other people do. You can't do all that partying. You can't sit back. When practice is over and everybody walks out of the gym, you can't walk out of the gym with them. You have to stay in here and work extra hard. If you want to be special, you've got to do the extra-special things. That's what's going to make you great." That was the one thing that I always tried to do. When everybody else is relaxing and trying to enjoy themselves, I still work. You've got to work when everybody else is playing. You've got to find fuel for your fire every day.

I read a lot of books—especially inspirational books. Books help you figure out what the world is about, what life is all about, and what it means to be in a certain place in your life. There are so many things that I've learned from reading books, so many different signs that I've seen, signs that have pushed me to the next level. I think everybody has these signs in their lives, but you have to realize that they're

there, and you have to be open-minded enough to see them and to know what your purpose in life is.

I've learned that the people I meet and the things I experience are in my life for a reason. I don't question it. I just take everything as it comes. Through books, I've learned that when you work hard to achieve your dream, the whole universe conspires to help you. And, that's kind of what my life has been like—from getting drafted to being in a movie. First, I put it in my mind. Then I worked toward it, and now it's not even on the horizon. It's right there. The dream is a reality.

Ambition is all you need to achieve superstardom. I get some of my passion through seeing how hard other people work. Other people may not necessarily be doing the things that you want to do, but they can help you develop the mentality you need because you see their passion. Whether they're in the business world or they're in another sport, I can see passion in others. I can see how hard they work, and I know that is why they are successful. I get some of my passion through seeing theirs. They inspire me.

A lot of kids look up to athletes and celebrities because they are on television, but nobody really knows the types of people we actually are. There are great athletes and there are some you would never want to have your kid around. The Ray of Hope Foundation is something I've established to give kids a *reason* to want to emulate some of the athletes. We do a lot of community activities, but most of all the foundation is for the kids. It's not for them to be with me, but a way for me to be with them. They need to know that people care about them and want to see them grow and become successful. I don't want them to end up in jail or dead at a young age. I believe in them. I want them to do great things with their lives and then extend that to their communities.

One of the things I tell them is that you have to believe in yourself. If you don't believe in yourself, nobody else is going to believe in you or understand your purpose. I tell them that as you grow up, no matter what you do or how much you achieve, there will always be people who will doubt you. As you get higher and as you get further up that ladder, people are going to continue to throw negative things at you, and they're going to refuse to believe in you. As long as you believe in yourself, and know that you can do it, you can keep walking up that ladder and moving to the top.

A man once asked me what I would be doing if I didn't play basketball. I told him I'd be playing baseball or football. He didn't believe me because he thought that I had been given the gift of basketball. I said, "No, I have not been given the gift of basketball. I've been given a gift, but the gift isn't basketball. The gift is the ability to work hard to achieve my goals. I'm not successful because I throw the basketball well. I'm successful because I have the discipline to go out there and work hard and adapt in order to be good."

Most people think that there is one way to do everything, that there's one main way to be successful, but that's not true. There are a lot of people who don't have the success that they dream of. But I say, just take your time. You will achieve greatness. I achieved a lot of my dreams at a very young age, but that is rare. Everybody's not going to do that, and everybody doesn't need to do that. Some people do it at thirty-five, some at forty-five, some not until eighty-five. You've got to take that patience and let it calm you, and grow you, and allow you to enjoy life. When you enjoy life, your passions come into play, and that's when you learn about yourself. If you have a passion for something, then money is not going to matter. And that's when you're going to be rolling in it. Learn to gain wisdom. Through wisdom you gain everything else. Sometimes when you come up against an obstacle, you think that it's over with. But it's never over with. It's just one door that's closed to you. When one door closes, another opens. You just have to find that other door.

nicole ari parker

Your soul tells you what to do.

the littlest things make us so beautiful. The things I love about acting are the things that we do as human beings that are just so beautiful. The way we look at somebody we love, the way we can't breathe when we're nervous, what shocks us, how we feel when our song comes on the radio. I love all the little things we do.

I believe in following your dreams, but sometimes, when it becomes difficult to live your dream, you realize that there's another dream underneath the first one. When people around me wanted to give up on a dream, I would say, "Don't give up! Don't give up." But if my friend who's a ballerina wants to stop dancing and become a singer, then I say, hang up the toe shoes.

Your soul tells you what to do and when to do it. But that doesn't mean it's ever time to do nothing. You have to search. Inside of everybody, there are gems. There's so much to share. If one thing is fading out, it may be time for another form of expression to start coming through. You have to know yourself, be yourself, and love yourself. It took me a long time to figure out what that meant. I'm so glad I did.

Even when I was a child, I wanted to be an actress. I'm your typical only child. I was very imaginative. I wrote plays, I acted all the characters, I made up songs, and I danced around the house. Nobody else in my family is involved in the entertainment industry, but they're all very dramatic, intense people. I developed a love of theater, a craving for the stage. At seventeen, I left Baltimore and came to New York University. In my second semester, I auditioned for NYU's Tisch School of the Arts and got in. My dad said, "Go for it!" And I did!

When I started auditioning, I took my passion for acting, my fervor, and my ambition into my auditions. It took me a minute to realize that people said no. I was like, "Why no?! What are you talking about, no? I can't have this job?" The waiting by the phone, the callbacks, the decisions, all that's involved in getting a part—how tall you are, how pretty you are, who's the costar, the packaging, the rejection—all of it started to take a toll on me.

My passion for performing got eaten away a little. I thought, *Why am I doing this?* A painter doesn't stop and ask somebody if they can paint, but acting is not a solitary art form. It requires other people. I had to go out into the world to seek my expression. As an artist, you feel that you have important things you have to express. When you feel that strongly, it's hard to put it in somebody else's hands. I had to do a lot of soul-searching. I couldn't skip over the audition process so I asked myself, "How do I make this holy?" I had to remind myself that this was something I loved, that I wanted to do, and that my passion belonged to me so that I didn't feel like people were taking it away from me all the time.

One movie that really influenced me was a French film called *The Passion of Joan of Arc.* It's a silent film I found in a video store one day. I didn't know much about St. Joan, but the description of the film was: The passionate fervor one woman has for God. I saw that, and I said, "Okay! I know that feeling!" Something about Renée Falconetti's face was just so familiar to me, so compelling. She gave me all this passion and conviction, and she has no lines! I just thought, *Wow! This is what I want to do! This is what it's all about!* It changed my life.

My film debut was an independent feature, *The Incredibly True Adventure of Two Girls in Love.* That was my first paying job and that was my first movie. I got it right after I quit my job at the Paramount Hotel. I had no money. I had just heard this voice saying, "You have just got to pursue your dreams." Ten days later, I got a leading role in *Two Girls in Love.*

As an actress, I'm very prepared. In addition to wanting to "live truthfully in imaginary circumstances," I always want to know: How does she talk? How does she walk? What does she wear? Where was she born? What's her favorite song, favorite color, favorite food? All of that. Where does she relate to me? The best work I've done has happened when it hits me on the inside. Even if you only understand one aspect of a part, one choice your character makes, you can figure out the rest. If one small thing can hit you in your heart about the character, then you've covered a lot and can make it all work.

I love what I do. As you rise in your career, you have to become multitalented. You've got to know how to work a room. You need to go to the party, go to the premiere, your dress has to be cute, your nails have to be done, your eyebrows have to be tweezed. Everything is part of the game. It was hard for me to do all of the other things, but I have learned to accept them as another part of acting.

It's been a long road, and I've always worked, but I didn't make any money until the series *Soul Food* came along. Everything's changing for me because in television, you've got to hit it and quit it. My technique has gone through a lot of changes because I have to speed up the process.

Of course, I would love for somebody to take me under their wing and tell me the secret of great acting. When I worked with Denzel on *Remember the Titans,* he told me not to overwork. Keep it simple.

It's important to be around people who are searching, people who are curious and keep you curious, people who inspire you to ask and answer questions. You've also always got to be around funny people, because life is funny.

Looking back, I wish I had been stronger. I wish I had generated more of my own work and experimented with my own ideas. There are empty theaters all over this city. I wish I had done a lot more writing, directing, and putting up plays on my own. It's never too late. People get so discouraged in this business, but you can't wait to be discovered. People who really wanted the responsibility and the power got there. They created opportunities for themselves. Spike Lee and Robert Townsend did it. Gina and Reggie Blythewood are doing it. Felicia O. Henderson is doing it.

I think we have to teach our kids to be fearless. When you bring up a kid to be fearless, they're less aggressive. When you teach them to pursue their goals, they're less threatened. If you teach a child that there ain't no work out there, no opportunities, you're perpetuating a myth that they're always going to be on the outside. You're teaching them very early to be desperate. But if you teach them that they will find work and not to be afraid to make mistakes, you teach them to change their minds and their lives.

The thing that excites me about the industry now is that we are allowing ourselves to blossom. We're not just putting up the same structures in blackface. We're accepting different kinds of music among ourselves, different hairstyles, different everything. We're not ashamed of ourselves or of each other. I'm excited about the new images that we are creating. We're revealing more. We're allowing ourselves to be more emotional, more human. I can remember being little and going to a movie, and if a brother cried onscreen, people mocked him. We couldn't handle it. Now we want that slow dolly close-up, we want to see the brother's pain. We are allowing a lot more of ourselves to shine through. As an actress, I am proud and excited about being part of that.

vivica a. fox

patience

*Things take time, but with a commitment to yourself and to your belief
in yourself, all things will come to pass.*

if you ever feel like you want to give up, just try a little bit harder. Things take
time. There will be a lot of rejection in any field that you have a desire to be in. But
with a commitment to yourself and to your belief in yourself, all things will come
to pass.

My biggest challenge is to maintain my balance and my vision. To stay humble.
To stay hungry. I'm a very ambitious person so I don't give up very easily. I just
keep trying, and I just keep trying, and I just keep trying. I've always kept my drive.

My mother taught me to believe in myself and my future. She was a great spiritual leader. She raised four children by herself and did a good job with us. She
kept us in school, kept us in church, and taught us very high morals, which you
need to survive in the entertainment industry. When I was a little girl growing up
in Indianapolis, I wanted to be a model. I wanted to be in the fashion and beauty
industry. After high school, I went to California and New York to try to be a model.
But everywhere I went, they basically told me, "Well, we've already got our token
Black girl." That was back in the day when only one Black person got in.

Believe it or not, acting just fell into my lap. I came back to California from New
York, in order to return to college in Orange County. One day, I went to Los Angeles to have lunch with my girlfriend, and this guy walked up to me and said, "So
you're an actress, right? You have a really good look." I said, "No, but I've modeled before." He told me, "Well, you should become an actress." He gave me his
card—no strings attached—got me an agent, and I started auditioning. His name

was Trevor Walton, and he was the guardian angel who opened the doors to my destiny, and I've been acting ever since.

It took me about three months to get my first job, which was a Clearasil commercial. From there I got soap operas, and the rest is history. My first break was *Generations*, which was the first integrated soap opera. After that I was on the series *Up All Night* with Patti LaBelle.

When *Up All Night* ended, I went through a period when I was not working. It was difficult, but I survived because I had wonderful support from my family, particularly my mother, who helped me maintain my faith on many different levels. I also received a lot of support from Sheila Willis, another one of my guardian angels. She is an actress I met on *Generations*. She had taken me under her wing and soon became my acting coach as well as my friend and mentor. Sheila told me, "Start working out, start taking care of yourself, because when an opportunity comes knocking at your door, if you're not ready you can't blame anybody but yourself." That was an important lesson for me to learn. Being patient doesn't mean being passive. In order to really have faith in tomorrow, you have to prepare yourself for success today. I started hiking, exercising, and taking care of myself physically and spiritually until I was finally at peace with myself. That's when I got *Independence Day,* which was my first experience of major movie stardom. Everything just started rolling after that.

If you're interested in acting, it's a good idea to enroll in some acting classes to see if you really want to do it because acting requires a lot of studying and a lot of hard work. A lot of people think, *Oh, I'm cute. I can be an actor.* But you have to take drama classes. You've got to learn what acting is all about. You've got to sharpen your craft, sharpen your tools. You do that by studying, taking care of yourself, working out, keeping your mind spiritually strong, really believing in yourself—and knocking on all kinds of doors.

It's tough getting used to the rejection, getting used to hearing "no" more than "yes." That skin just has to get a little thick, and you have to know that maybe that role just wasn't meant for you. Sometimes it's political. Sometimes it has nothing to do with you. Sometimes it's just not your turn. I worked. I continued to work odd jobs on the side so I had a little money. But I made sure that I was available during the day to go and audition and to go knock on those doors.

The best part of being an actress is working with incredible talent and the satisfaction of doing a good film. The hardest part is staying on top. Finding those good roles. The opportunities are limited, but the future of Hollywood is exciting for us as Black people. For once we're creating our own paths, our own projects, writing, directing, producing, being in control of our own destiny.

I love stories about women standing up for themselves and each other so I'm glad I've been able to do films like *Set It Off* and *Soul Food* that really explore those kinds of relationships. *Waiting to Exhale* by Terry Macmillan is one of my all-time favorite books. I was really happy to see it brought to the screen because it's a story of togetherness—of women's empowerment and of women sticking together. That book really encouraged and inspired me.

I truly enjoy being a role model for young African-American girls. I want to let them know that the color of your skin cannot hold you back. You were blessed with color. Enjoy it, and know that you're a child of God. He shines on you, too. You're just as beautiful as anyone else.

It's fun and exciting living out my dream. I am having a wonderful time. I'm meeting some of the most incredible people and working with the best of the best. It's just a wonderful life, and I don't take it for granted. I see myself as a hard-working soul sister who's very blessed to have made it. I absolutely love what I do.

suzanne de passe

paying dues

You are not defined by getting the coffee, licking the stamps, or making the copies. You are only defined by your attitude about getting the coffee, licking the stamps, or making the copies. There is no substitute—none—for paying dues.

i have learned that you must be aware at all times of whether or not you are moving in the direction of your goals and desires. We are all the captains of the ships that we sail—our lives. We cannot be the slightest bit timid about asserting ourselves and making choices that put us in a better place—a place closer to our goals. It is very difficult when you are starting off because you don't have a lot of credits or a strong sense of knowing how to do things. But the one thing I learned was that there is no substitute—none—for paying dues.

Today I look back on that first decade of my career, and I think, *But for that, I would not be able to do anything today,* because it was so important to learn from the ground up. It was so important to be mentored by Berry Gordy. It was so important to work around the creative excellence of what Motown was and what Motown meant. It was vital. All these years later, I really believe that I approach my career with the same kind of intensity that was present in those early Motown years. The lessons of those early years have continued to guide me in tremendously powerful ways.

As a young person, I was always very industrious. I was a reader. I was a writer. I was a dreamer. I always felt that I would be successful at something. I always nurtured this spark because I knew I had something to say. Life is peculiar because I don't know that anybody ever gets exactly where they thought they were going to go. When I was a teenager, I thought I was going to be a writer. I was in college studying English when I became interested in the music business. I was working as a talent coordinator at a dance hall in New York City when I met the people from Motown.

My first job at Motown was as creative assistant to Berry Gordy. It was very strange to go from college dropout to having an office and a secretary while I was still a teenager. I set out on a career at a time when very, very few women were in major positions of influence and power in the record business. At that point, I was so happy to be in the room where things were going on that it didn't occur to me that I was a sort of pioneer. I was very intent on learning as much as I could. It was exciting, and I was thriving on the opportunity that was there, but I was also weeping at how hard it was. That struggle has paid off because when it was time to start my own company, I knew how to make it succeed.

One thing Berry Gordy told me early on was that there's no job too big and no job too small. I really think that that speaks to a larger issue—which is that attitude is everything. People often don't realize that you are not defined by getting the coffee, licking the stamps, making the copies, or any of that stuff. You are only defined by your attitude about getting the coffee, licking the stamps, or making the copies. If your attitude is that there is no job too big and no job too small, then you are liberated from the pettiness of what so much of professional life can be. Many people don't realize that it is better to be in an entry-level position in an environment that brings you close to what you want to do than to work as a vice-president of something you hate or that you don't want to do for a long time. In other words, there's a difference between a career and a job, and too many people take jobs.

You must strive to always be around people who are smarter than you are, who know more than you know, and who will share with you. You must never work for people who are petty or people who mean you ill will. Sometimes we must do what we must do, but we have to stay awake and remain focused on our goals. Overall, I think that it's a tremendously satisfying, invigorating, wonderful experience to work in a creative industry, where ideas are the currency. The alchemy of creativity is satisfying in and of itself. You get to do wonderful things, meet incredible people, and oh! by the way, you get paid to do it. It's a fine profession.

You're always a little bit scared, but I think passion overcomes fear. When you're passionate about something, you're afraid, you're concerned, but you're also excited. If passion is what is driving you, then fear has to take a backseat to that passion as you push past it. If your fear is greater than your passion, then you shouldn't be doing what you're doing. Learn from what life hands you. Experience is such a great teacher. That may be a cliché, but it's a cliché because it's true. The mistakes that I've made have been whoppers, but they have been my best teachers in some ways. It's more important to say, "I'm not asleep at the wheel. I'm not just going through the motions. I don't have it to do over again, but I have tomorrow—it's not necessarily promised, but if it comes, I'll do better because I'm learning and growing."

The great thing about dreaming is that as you achieve one dream, you get to dream new ones. I always have a dream handy, and I've been blessed to have realized so many of my dreams. As I progress, I am always delighted that life has proven to me that so many things are possible. I wouldn't dare to not have a dream. I, by nature, am a dreamer. I've always got one in my hip pocket.

I also feel very strongly that we have to help young people nurture their dreams as we continue to nurture ours. We do need to reach back and share the knowledge that we have. It's flattering when I hear that there are young people who want to be the next me, but I would say that they should aspire to be better than I am. Stand on my shoulders, learn from my knowledge and experience, but find your unique gifts and express them. The goal is not to become the next anybody. The goal is to become the best version of yourself.

phylicia rashad

potential

We must learn and reach from a source of creativity—that wellspring of expression—because once we drink of those waters, our vision changes and we become free.

as human beings, we have capacities that are much greater than we imagine them to be. A lot of times what happens with people—especially young people—is that they never get to experience their own depth. If you never have an experience of your depth, not even a glimpse of it, you don't understand who you are, your own ability. You don't *understand* your potential so it's difficult to live up *to* your potential. Today there are so many students and so few people who are there for them to say, "Oh, no, no, darling, you are *not* a hoochie mama. You are a high priestess. No, no, baby, that's not what you do. No, no, sweetheart, that's not what your body is for. Your body is a temple, darling. Why? Because of the one who is living in it." There are not a lot of people who give young people a glimpse of their depth. If we don't change that, who will?

When I was a little girl, Jim Crow laws were in full effect. Jim Crow laws were the laws that legalized segregation in this country. That meant Black people couldn't work in certain places, that we had inferior schools, separate water fountains, and that we had to sit in the back of the bus, both literally and on every other level. Most young Black people can't even imagine what it was like, but there are those of us who still remember. What people have to say about African-Americans in the film industry today, of course, is true—but, honey, it was truer then. There's always been something good going on, but in spurts. It's like a wheel, and we need to get off! We need to learn from these things, get off this wheel, and stop going around and

around and around. Is it a question of *just* learning from the past, or is it more a question of learning about ourselves? I think it's about that essence of ourselves that is not touched by time, that is not dependent on external circumstances and is unaffected by them. We must learn and reach from a source of creativity—that wellspring of expression—because once we drink of those waters, our vision changes and we become free.

It's necessary to surround yourself with people who support you in what you're doing, who encourage and inspire you. For me, the most important inspiration was my mother. My mother is really the one. *The* one. My mother included us in everything she did. We learned to respect other people's space, to respect other people's needs, and to respect other people's work. She taught me to read music when I was five years old and I never forgot it. I play piano, guitar, and viola. I sing, and for years I have done musical theater. She was not a materialistic woman. She gave us what we needed. She had us running around saying things like "The universe bears no ill toward me; I bear no ill toward it." She would wake us up in the morning saying, "Be bold! Be beautiful, be free." Oh, yes, she's incredible. She put the development of our human capabilities above anything else, much to the chagrin of many of the ladies of the community. They used to look at us out of the corner of their eyes and they'd say, "Vivienne is not rearing those children right. She just lets them say what they think and they just run wild. They'll never amount to anything." But my mother knew better. I'm living a wonderful life. My sister is Debbie Allen. In the end, her children thrived because of the freedom and encouragement she gave us.

I remember being a little child playing in the elephant ear plants in Houston, pretending I was Sheena, Queen of the Jungle. I knew that she really should have looked more like me than she did on TV. But I was not yet thinking of becoming an actress. That changed when I was eleven years old. I was auditioning to read a libretto for a piece of music that was going to be the climax of a great musical festival in Houston. Each school prepared a student to read. When I finished auditioning, they invited me to be the mistress of ceremonies for the entire evening. Now at eleven years old, I considered myself very ugly and very gawky. Everybody in my family was beautiful, and I just thought, *Oh, God must have been taking a lunch break when I came through.* But I learned my script so well that I knew it by heart.

I'd never stood in the spotlight before, but there I was standing in the spotlight, dressed in this beautiful little yellow and white dress. I had white flowers in my hair, and curls, and white socks with ruffles on them. I just stood there, and talked to the light, which is all I could see, and I did my best. When the festival was over and people were leaving the Coliseum, I heard several mothers say, "Oh, there she is. There's the little girl who spoke so beautifully. Isn't she beautiful?" I heard that, and I thought, *That's it. When I grow up, I'm going to be an actress. I'll play in the light, and I'll be beautiful all of the time.*

What I couldn't articulate then, but had truly experienced, was the beauty of communicating from one's own heart. That's what being an actress means to me. I went on to study music and theater at Howard University. My mother sent me to New York after my sophomore year with money she had been saving for a year. That experience of working in New York opened many, many doors for me.

The best advice I could give to someone else is to study. Study with a master. The great teacher is the one who unlocks the knowledge inside the student, who helps you open the door inside yourself, and delivers you to yourself. The great teacher isn't one who just teaches you. The great teacher liberates you.

I have made a strong commitment to a spiritual path. I realized that God is the great actor of the universe. He's playing many parts, and He's the star of the show. With this knowledge, I began to realize that I had not correctly understood the work that I was pursuing as an actress. All concerns about what somebody was going to think, what the producer was going to say, whether the critics were going to like it, what the audience was going to think—all of that went away because it wasn't about me anymore. It was not about proving one's self or displaying one's self anymore. No. This work is an offering. Once I began to understand my work as an offering, it was total freedom.

Before that, when I would prepare for a role, I was bound up like a ball of yarn. I would wonder, *Am I going to get it right? Am I going to feel that inspiration?* I began to understand that my own self is the source of inspiration. I understood that in order to give a real offering, I had to focus on that self. That doesn't mean that you don't do your preparation. Let's not be silly. What it meant was that I had to offer the work to that quiet space within my own being because that is the space we all share. That's how to live in the world properly—by following your path truthfully and offering the fruits of your efforts. You offer the work, and you do it without concern of what will come back to you. Just be grateful for the work itself. Your work is the thing to be grateful for.

People talk about the twenty-first century as something so mysterious because we have become so automated and computerized. But don't the plants still need to be watered? Don't the children still need to be raised? The most important thing is seeing my children through. We need to see all of our children through, and we can do that by loving them, by taking time to be with them, by respecting them and their need to grow, and by respecting their need to experience their own depth.

n'bushe wright

Train a lot. Go to school and train till you're blue in the face.

i was a loner, and I was always searching for something. I wasn't necessarily finding it in people, but I think I was finding it in training. Dance technique had a tremendous impact on me as an actress and as a person. It gave me stamina and it gave me a certain strength. Dance prepared me for success.

You have to be strong in this business. You can't just be an entertainer. You have to be ready psychologically. You have to be ready mentally. You have to be ready physically. When I started out, I was always trying to be the best that I could be, and I was training in the meantime. I was always trying to be on my game. I go to church. I have a relationship with God. I try to stay strong—strong spiritually—by keeping my craft and my body together.

If I had children, I would tell them to go to school and to train in whatever they wanted to do. I definitely think it's important to be in a creative and artistic environment. And just train a lot. Go to school and train till you're blue in the face.

when I was a little girl, I thought I wanted to be a dancer, but eventually, I turned from dancing to acting. Both of my parents are from Brooklyn, from Bedford-Stuyvesant, and I was raised by both my mother and my father. Growing up, my favorite movie was *Black Orpheus* and my favorite actress was Pam Grier. Definitely. I wanted to be Pam Grier when I grew up.

The person who had the most influence on my career was my mother. She influenced me by example because she was always working really hard and she was always in college. She was just always motivated. I would see her get up and exercise in the morning. She fought to get me in some of the more specialized schools. It was a great example for me, just seeing her motivation to keep learning.

i had studied at Alvin Ailey, Martha Graham, and the High School for the Performing Arts. I was becoming interested in acting so after school, I started studying at some of the acting programs in New York like the Stella Adler Acting Conservatory.

In the beginning I just worked. I was trying so hard just to make it, and I never stopped to ask myself what the hardest thing was because everything was hard. Everything was hard, and it was just, like, "I can't stop, I can't stop, I can't stop." When something got easy, it was, like, "Oh." I made it hard again because I didn't even understand ease. I've always felt like I'm doing ten million things.

Zebrahead was my first job. I didn't have a job before *Zebrahead*. I never acted before *Zebrahead*. The director said that what he liked the most about working with children is that they weren't "acting." And he just tried to remind us because he thought we were close enough in our youth to remember what it was like to be a child and not to have technique in acting—to just be.

I'm nervous every time I audition. I'm still nervous because you have to show a very vulnerable side of yourself. You have to open up, and if you're not appreciated, then you feel a bit rejected. When I started out, and I didn't get a part, I don't know if I thought of it as rejection as much as I thought of it as my having to get better.

i'm a method actress so as soon as I get the role, I basically become the character. And I find that at night I dream the character. As an actress, if you're constantly working, you're always in this fantasy place. You're so used to making up other worlds. But when I leave the real world, I get into trouble. In order to have a meaningful life, you have to become a real person again, at least for a little while.

I've always hoped that real life would give me the experience for the work that I do. I think it's up to each actor to bring an integrity to the role, but I find that the roles that they have Black women going for sometimes can be a little exploitive. But sometimes I've felt like *Oh, am I representing Black women in the right way?* It got really hard and at a certain point you feel like, *I just want to go to college. I want to have a family and be simple. I just want to be regular old folk.* But then I realized that this is what I am. I have no idea about any of that other stuff. This is something that God has given me, and it's very natural. It's by His grace. This is the most natural thing that I've ever done in my whole life, and it's something that I've trained for my whole life. I am an actress.

music has really inspired me—it is an incredible backdrop for inspiration and for your characters and for scenes. My brother is a producer and he has also really influenced me because of his connection to hip-hop. I've realized that adults in our communities may respond to religious leaders, but children respond to hip-hop and television and movies so I do have a responsibility to come out and say, "This is wrong." Or "This is right." Or "You can make it if you do this." If each of us in entertainment made some kind of effort—whether it's being a big sister, teaching a dance class to a group of high school students, or just going back to our communities to do one small thing—it would make a huge difference. I think it is extremely important for us to be active in the community.

In the end, it's up to each of us to make our own choices. We have no idea what's gonna happen tomorrow, but it's up to us to decide our destiny. We make our own destiny. That really is the most exciting thing about life.

malik yoba

purpose

I'm deeply passionate about the idea of mastering something. I strive for a certain level of ecstasy in performance. It's like being suspended in a place of truth—not necessarily your truth, but the truth of that moment. My choices are based on purpose.

i'm deeply passionate about the idea of mastering something—the ability to look at a situation and see how things are going to develop. I love acting. I strive for a certain level of ecstasy in performance. It's like being suspended in a place of truth—not necessarily your truth, but the truth of that moment. And sometimes it is also your truth because you're basing it on what you're performing and what you've experienced. You can do something meaningful with what you have learned.

I've learned that success breeds success. If you have people who are successful in your life as a child, they will help breed that in you. My drive was fostered by my parents. They motivated me to try to achieve greatness and to do great things, to never be mediocre. They let me know that it was available to me if I wanted it, and if I was willing to work for it. So it starts there. Then when you have your own successes as an individual, that breeds more success in your life.

Life is no rehearsal. This is not a trivial matter here—this is for real. I know a lot of people can't deal with the political realities, but I just feel that dealing with them is part of my purpose. That's one of the reasons I'm involved in media, in technology, film, television, and music. I have to use the media and use my energy to affect my environment. I'm on it. I know I can do well and do good at the same time. I'm just trying to follow my path. My choices aren't based on stardom—they are based on purpose.

i was born and raised in New York. The city raised me. I have five siblings, and we are very close. We wrote plays as kids, and I always looked at that as my start. We grew up without a television, so we had to write plays to entertain ourselves. Even now all of us are excellent writers. I remember the magic of theater as a kid. Because we didn't grow up with television, we didn't have anything feeding our minds other than life itself.

I saw the play *Alice in Wonderland* when I was four years old, and I was completely blown away by the lighting, the costumes, and the drama. I identified with it because even at that age, I was involved in making costumes and scenery for the plays we did at my house. I just remember seeing that play and feeling—*I have to do this.*

I actually gave my autograph to my teachers when I was thirteen and told them that one day I was going to be famous and that they should keep it. I had a lot of interests. People used to tell me, "You need to get focused." But to me, I *was* focused—I was focused on what I was doing and I was doing it.

when I was twenty-three, I met a guy who was producing Broadway plays and music. He had all these things, and I asked him, "What do you do?" He said, "I'm a brew master. I stir it up, I get things started, and then I move on to the next project." I was, like, "That's me."

it takes a lot of work to live out this idea of stardom and to maintain this idea that you are *so* important. You can't be yourself anymore. You have to have security around you. You have to maintain a certain image. You have to wear sunglasses at night. You have to give interviews. You have to wear sexy outfits. You have to do all these things to maintain it. But that's not what makes you important. It's not about fame. I never did it for fame.

We sustain our stars because the people believe in us. The reality is that my "star" is sustained by the community because they were the people I was always trying to reach, and they understood that. They have never withdrawn their support.

i still believe that we need to focus on global understanding, to recognize the interconnectedness of everyone and use technology to help humanity catch up with itself. We have surpassed ourselves on some levels with technology, because we have gadgets that do so many things that we don't really need. But we still have racial wars and all of these other ills.

I'm really excited about where we are now culturally and artistically. There are so many young people of color doing their thing. I am excited by the possibility that more of us will be on an even playing field. World politics is about money and power, and perception. I think that more people of color are learning to use the idea of cooperative economics in the right way so that things can really change. There's so much more to be learned not only from an educational standpoint, but also from how we live together as a society.

lynn whitfield

refinement

*Quality is important. No matter what you are doing, your standard of
presentation to the world should always stay at a certain level.*

a star is a luminous body that shares its light. Being a star is really all about illu-
mination, illuminating something other than yourself. For me, it means bringing
light to my work so that when people see me, they can sense that I have a heart,
can sense that I pray and that I love God. It also means that there is a responsibility involved in celebrity that includes very simple things like never lowering your
standards. My family helped me understand this. Often that means that I have not
been working because I have to put my foot down and say, "No! I am not going
to do these things that I think work against my vision!" No matter what you are
doing, your standard of presentation to the world should always stay at a certain
level. I try to stay focused on that.

louisiana and my family have powerfully informed my life and work. Louisiana
is one of the most interesting states in the Union. It carries a lot of tradition and
wonder, and it carries a lot of baggage because it was a major port but it was also
where the slave ships came. With all of that comes a lot of history, and a lot of it
filters into the families that live there. A lot of what I experienced was wonderful
so I think that when people look at me, and they respect or admire me, it is because I was formed by all that was extraordinary about my family. But at the same
time, a lot of what I use in my work is the pain, the things that do not make me feel
good. I try to share the complexity of dealing with issues like rejection, betrayal,
disappointment, or loss, which was also informed by my family. They gave me

tremendous gifts, and every year that you get older and do all the healing and for-giving, you realize that your parents and your family are only doing the best that they can, just like you. Every year, I'm just more grateful for the gifts I was given.

my mother was extremely glamorous. I mean, Elizabeth Taylor, Marilyn Monroe, Jackie Kennedy, it didn't matter. I would just turn around and there was Mom. She represented all of that. I was also very close to my grandmother, who gave me the most gentle, yielding love.

She loved old movies so I grew up watching the late movies with her. Unfortunately, there weren't many people of color to see, but Dorothy Dandridge seemed to encompass everything I liked because she was a femme fatale. I didn't know all of the tragedy she endured, I just knew that she was beautiful, she was glamorous, her acting was dramatic, and she was accepted, or so we thought, from afar. From Baton Rouge, Louisiana, it looked like she had it all going on, so I was very influenced by her.

My father always knew that it was great to expose us to things. So when I was thirteen, he brought me to New York City because he had a song called "Dream of a Time" that was being performed at Carnegie Hall. I heard my father's song performed by Donald Shirley and then we went to a party and I met Brock Peters, and Leontyne Price, and Cicely Tyson, who was the toast of New York. I still remember her afro, and the suit she was wearing. I met all of these people and it was, *Yes!* Because they were doing what I wanted to do. I was very inspired by people who were already doing what I wanted to do, and I still am to this day.

So I went into formal theater training at Howard University and at the DC Black Reperatory Company, where I studied hard, stayed up late into the night, did acting workshops, and got to do experimental theater. When I graduated, I toured with a Black version of *The Taming of the Shrew,* and I became a member of the international touring company of *For Colored Girls* with Alfre Woodard and Mary Alice. It was a great group of women and everybody came to see that show, including people from Columbia Pictures who asked me to be a part of a training program and I got a contract. After that, I just started hustling, and I really began to understand that Audrey Hepburn, Bette Davis, Marilyn Monroe, and Susan Hayward were white, and that it was different for me. I wasn't being called upon to do anything glamorous.

I started studying with David LeGrant, a teacher who really taught me how to share myself through my work and through any character that I took on. Many people don't know my acting teacher, but for me he's the best. Quality is important. You should surround yourself with the best of everything, but the best does not necessarily mean well-known.

I actually think we can best influence the next generation by being bearers of light. Black people who have managed to be successful need to keep walking the walk and remember that our power, accomplishment, and purpose cannot influence people if they cannot connect to us. It is important to continue to be available in some way so that people can see you, feel that they can touch you, and believe that they can attain the same level of achievement. It's up to each person to figure out how they can be tangible to the African-American community so that people know that you care and that their dreams are as possible as yours.

For me, the actual craft of acting is a joy. When you're an actor, all you have is what's from the ends of your hair to the ends of your toes. That's it. You don't have anything else. You are your only commodity. I was formed by watching actresses who did not have certain kinds of limitations, and I want African-American actresses to have those same opportunities.

as a woman, I am moving into new phases. It will be fascinating to see how I will maneuver through an industry that says your career is over at twenty-eight. It is important to me that I move through that and stay with what I have—my purpose, and my path, and my sensuality. I'm not ready to put on the flowered dress and just be everybody's mother. There are some good, good, good love scenes left in me and I'm going to have them! Sometimes people think I've already arrived, but I have so many dreams. I have so many things that I still want to accomplish. I am a work in progress.

It is very important to me that I am a full-grown woman, a good woman with a good life, which means that my child is good, my relationship is good, and my business is good. If you read Proverbs, it's amazing how the Bible describes a woman as virtuous because she is handling everything. Everything! She is a great businesswoman, her children are happy, her husband's happy. It is a lot of hard work.

When I did *Josephine Baker*, I saw that she had made such unwise decisions that she had to try to backpedal and catch up with her destiny. I realized that I don't ever want to look back over my life and feel that I deserted the woman in me, or the artist in me. I want to embrace them both and make the most of both of them. In the end, I hope that I am remembered as a good woman with a great talent who made the most of the gifts she was given, and who kept God as part of her life.

vanessa williams

resilience

*It's only when you learn how to struggle and survive that you discover
who you really are. What's important has nothing to do with how you
look on the outside. It has to do with the strength, the vision, and the
gifts that motivate and sustain you from within.*

it's only when you learn how to struggle and survive that you discover who you
really are. You learn lessons in life when you have to feel it in your heart the hard
way, and experience it the hard way, as opposed to really not knowing pain or not
knowing embarrassment or disaster. People are always under the misconception
that if you're considered beautiful, you have no problems. But what's important
has nothing to do with how you look on the outside. It has to do with the strength,
the vision, and the gifts that motivate and sustain you from within.

In this industry, when you're bankable and you make money, it doesn't seem
to matter who you are and what you are capable of. Opportunity initially comes
from people being able to make money off of you, but longevity comes from being consistent and professional and having talent. Staying in the game is all
about talent.

my parents are both music teachers so our house was always filled with music. I always knew that I wanted to dance and be onstage. My goal was to be an
Alvin Ailey dancer because my mother would take me to see Alvin Ailey every
season. I've actually been dancing my whole life, longer than I've been singing.
I have been in dance classes since I was about five years old.

in high school, we had a drama department. I was a finalist for a drama scholarship from the National Endowment of the Arts so it's not like I was singing and decided to start acting. I'd acted pretty much through everything. But the roles just got better and better. I studied musical theater in college at Syracuse University, and I continue to benefit from the training I received there and from my parents.

i never planned to be Miss America. I wanted to be a stage actress. I was recruited for the Miss America Pageant because they would come up on campus and go watch the shows and then ask the girls whether they wanted to be involved. At that point I think they had seen me in three shows and I had said, "No! No! No!" And finally at the end of the year, a show that I was supposed to be in was canceled and I had free time, so I did it.

If I could do it all over again, I wouldn't have allowed myself to be recruited. I would have stayed with my original plan. I would have graduated college at Syracuse, and then gone to Yale Drama School, and then to New York to become a theater actor—and who knows what would have happened after that.

I became Miss America when I was twenty so I have been dealing with fame since then. Being Miss America was like celebrity boot camp for me. There was no public relations person telling you what to do or how to handle things or when to cut things off. The Miss America program is a very local mom-and-pop kind of operation, as opposed to the slick machine that most people think it is. In terms of dealing with media sharks, they had never had such attention before, because I was the first Black ever to receive the title. I think that was really the shocker, and getting through those first two years or so was what made me tough. Now, nothing can really phase me.

When I didn't get the support that I wanted from the Miss America pageant, I decided to resign before it got any worse. At that point, I pursued the dreams that I had put on hold while I was Miss America. That dream was to become an actress and do musical theater.

After the pageant, I got sidetracked, but I was never defeated. I was only twenty-one at the time so I had plenty of years to accomplish my goal. During that time, it was a long process of recording and television work and small parts in film and doing some theater out in LA and New York, and working my way up to my goal. It took ten years to finally achieve my original goal of having a leading role on Broadway. What happened during the pageant was difficult, but it never took away my voice or my desire.

i've always admired Lena Horne. I had always thought she was beautiful, but when I was studying musical theater in college, I began to really admire her work and her life. As an adult, I've continued to rediscover her legacy. So I remember the first time I met her I was almost speechless, and she said, "It's all right, baby. It's all right." She was very maternal and just an exquisite beauty. She calmed me down and made me not feel like a fool, because I was thinking, *Oh my God. I just love you.* It's so inspiring when you hear her life story. She had a very tough road, and she's paved the way for many of us who are in the industry now.

Despite my successes, I'm still a Black woman in an industry where you have to fight for a role. You're constantly trying to convince people that this woman could be any woman. She doesn't have to be a White woman. She could be a woman of color.

Fortunately, there are many more Black films that are being made by Black producers and directors, and we're basically creating our own opportunities, which is fantastic.

i think it's important to have people who believe in you. My parents always supported me. They said, "Do whatever you want, but be good at it." I try to instill those same values in my children. I let them know that they don't have the option of *not* going to school. You're going to college. So I try to find out what they are really interested in. One loves fashion, so we talk about schools with fashion departments and gearing her life to do that. One loves animals and wants to be a marine biologist. So we talk about schools with great marine biology departments. Their goals might change, but they already know that not going to college is simply *not* an option, and I think it motivates them to really figure out what their dreams are.

i'm an optimist. I still believe that people are genuinely good. I think you have to give kids the freedom to be themselves so that they can learn from their own mistakes. Being an overprotective parent doesn't necessarily make you have better children because they never get a chance to be responsible and learn things on their own.

Most of my decisions come from gut instinct, and from knowing that having to make choices is actually an important part of the blessings that you receive. I would love to continue to be happy and to have the choices that I do have, so I never feel like I'm forced into doing anything. I always want to have options because success means having the freedom to do what really inspires you.

terry mcmillan

resourcefulness

One thing I learned is that even under the worst circumstances,
the truth still works.

i have always been interested in having a positive impact on people, particularly African-Americans. I wanted to be able to tell stories that depicted us in an accurate manner, even if they weren't always flattering. I wanted to tell stories that we would be able to at least learn something from, without being didactic. The process is what helps you discover things. One thing I've discovered is that even under the worst circumstances, the truth still works.

My first job was working in a community library in Michigan. I think that had a lot to do with my appreciation of and introduction to not just literature but the world. The way you learned about the world in the 60s was boring history, and it was all White history—you saw the world through their eyes. At the library, I got to see world the way I wanted to, and I loved it.

When I was a child, I didn't know what I wanted to be. All I knew is I wanted to get out of my hometown, I wanted to go to college, and I did not want to be a housewife or a welfare mother and end up in the projects like a lot of people I knew. It wasn't until I was in college that I started to figure out what I wanted to do.

I wrote a poem by accident in college. I was living in Los Angeles when my roommate's friend Eric came over. My little poem was on the kitchen table, and he said, "Who wrote this poem?" I was annoyed because I thought that he was being nosy, but I told him, "I wrote it." And he said, "Can I publish it?" It turned out that he had just started a literary quarterly at the college. I thought he was joking about publishing it, but he did. From that day forward, honey, I thought I was a poet. I mean, I was writing some poetry. I couldn't go to the bathroom without writing poetry. I was writing. So that's sort of how it started.

I transferred to UC Berkeley where I used to love to write term papers and editorials for campus papers. I was going to declare sociology as my major, but I had to talk to my adviser first. My adviser said, "Why sociology?" And I said, "Because I want to save the world." And he said, "How?" And I told him, "That's why I want to major in sociology. I want to find out how. Even if I can't change the whole world, just a small corner of it would do. A few people. Myself included." He said, "That's very good but what about those articles I've read of yours? Don't you find writing gratifying?" I said, "Yeah, but it's just a hobby." He asked me, "Why is it that people always think that the things that they enjoy the most can only be a hobby?" And I answered, "My mama told me I gotta make a living." Well, he told me that there are a lot of writers who make a living. Then he told me to go home, think about why I like to write, and come back and declare my major. I came back and declared my major as journalism.

After college, there were a lot of gray years when I was doing a lot of partying. I realized that I had the potential to become a drug addict, like everybody else I knew. Then I said to myself, "Hold on a minute, Terry. I did not go to Berkeley for this. I've got a brain, and I'll be damned if I'm gonna fry it." I applied to Columbia University film school and went to New York. I planned to stay two years, and ended up staying ten.

I had a baby, I was working as a word processor at a law firm to pay my bills, and I was doing writing workshops with the Harlem Writer's Guild. They were very encouraging and nurturing. It was there that I wrote a short story that became *Mama,* my first novel. I was thirty-two when I started writing it, and it I sold over 9,000 copies with no advertising. My publisher did no advertising. I did it myself.

When *Mama* was coming out, the publisher said, "Oh, we love the book, we absolutely love it, love it." Then all these white writers were coming out at the same time, and I'd read about their sixteen-city book tours and talk show appearances. So I said, "Am I going on any talk shows? How many cities am I going to?" And they said, "We don't really have a budget for you to go on a tour." And I said, "What?!"

I've always been a resourceful person so I bought some books and taught myself about marketing. I became my own publicist. There are a lot of really great books about the publishing industry. They tell you everything—how to write a query letter, how to write a proposal, whom to approach and how to approach an agent or a publisher, all of it. New writers should know the value of research and preparation.

I sent one-page letters about my book to the head buyer of every major bookstore chain, every Black bookstore, every college bookstore, and to every institution with a reading series. I wrote them on the computer at work and took them home. My son was just a baby, but he would wet envelopes or throw them in the shopping bag. Next day, I'd drop them off in the mailroom. The brothers in the mailroom didn't charge me a thing for that mail. I just said, "When the book comes out, I'll give you a copy." There was a sister who was my supervisor, and she knew what I was doing. But they were so proud that I was doing something with my life that they let me get away with it. I mailed out over 3,000 letters.

One day, the president of my publishing company called me up to tell me that they had sold out the first printing of the book. He also told me that the president of Barnes & Noble had called him to congratulate me on my initiative. He said, "The regional representatives liked her letter, and they liked her book. That girl's got a lot of nerve, but we need more like her because if we had depended on you guys, we would never even have known about the book." The company publicist who was in charge said that she would never, under any circumstances, work with me on my next book, and I said that's fine because she didn't work with me on the first one. By the time my book was published in 1987, it was already in its fourth printing, and I had so many reading invitations that I quit my job. A lot of Black writers have book tours and decent publicity now, and I think I had a whole lot to do with it. That's one thing I will take credit for.

During this time *Mama* helped me win a number of writing fellowships that sent me on writing workshops. It was in those workshops that I wrote *Disappearing Acts.* Later I wrote *Waiting to Exhale,* which they called my breakthrough book, although I'm proud of the success of all of my books. One thing I was not prepared for was fame. One thing I get a lot is, "Has anybody ever told you that you look a lot like Terry McMillan? Does it get on your nerves when people say that?" I say, "Yes, it does because she is older than I am. Plus, I don't think she is all that cute, so am I supposed to be flattered?" I just play it up.

Of course, I always fantasized about what it would be like to be a bestselling author. Every author does. But that was not my motivation for writing. I believe that when people read a book, any book, I don't care what the subject is, they should be changed somehow. People should be uplifted after opening a book, based on what they've learned and discovered as a result of reading it. There has to be some little gem that they might discover, some strength that somebody has that might affect them or change them. I never wished or prayed for fame. Ever. All I ever wanted was respect. I wanted people to read my books, and, hopefully, to be moved by them.

eriq la salle

respect

Don't be an artist because you want to. Be an artist because you have to. Professional art is not a recreational commitment

i love my life, and I love being an actor. In the arts, you are always learning about your past. People look at me and they talk about the success that I've achieved on TV, but it wasn't just me. There were a bunch of actors who came before me. They were more talented than I am, more versatile, better looking. They just did not have the same opportunities that I have. I'm not the most brilliant actor to ever come along. I just came along at the right time, and that time was created by the people before me. It was my responsibility to be prepared for when that time presented itself, just like it's this generation's or the next generation's responsibility to make sure that they're prepared when opportunities present themselves to them. Teaching them that lesson is the best thing we can give them. You have to understand that it's a process—a collective process. It's one generation creating opportunities for their generation and the next generation. When you know that, you understand not only your agenda but also your responsibility. It ain't just about you.

I have to thank all of the people who made it possible. People I don't know, people I've never heard of, people I've never seen. They are great artists because they took a stand even if they weren't allowed to have a career. I have sincere respect—and I mean truly, truly heartfelt, sincere respect—for the people who created these opportunities for me. I know I'm not the best actor in the world, but I know I respect my craft, and I respect the people who made it possible for me to be an artist.

The greatest challenge in my career is coping with the disrespect of my craft. Everyone feels acting is easy, that they don't need to go to school for it, that they don't need to study the craft. That lack of respect is made worse by the "isms"—the everyday racism, sexism, and ageism that you face in this business. One thing that was instilled in me is—don't be an artist because you want to. Be an artist because you *have* to. Become an actor because your spirit would not be whole if you didn't. My spirit would be absolutely incomplete if I didn't do what I do. That's why I have problems with people who do this recreationally. Professional art is not a recreational commitment.

In my mind, I'm a skinny bow-legged kid from Hartford, Connecticut. If you look at all the statistics, I'm not supposed to be here. I grew up with people who are in jail. I grew up with people who are drug addicts. I grew up with people who are dead now. The statistics are overwhelmingly in favor of me ending up like that as opposed to me growing up in a small, predominantly Black neighborhood and going on to fulfill my dream. Every day that I'm here, every opportunity that I have, is a blessing.

My mother had a tremendous impact on me and not just the obvious impact that a mother has on a child. She influenced me by defining herself as a hero because of all the obstacles she had overcome. I was able to see myself in the mirror of her life, a life of incredible hardship, but one in which she stayed true to who she was. She had this incredible faith system that really helped shape who I am today. I ultimately wanted to be an actor because of Sidney Poitier. He had this commanding sense of dignity before I even knew what the word dignity meant. The power of that dignity infused me with a positive sense of my own potential, and that made me want to act.

I got where I am by the traditional route. I respect the process of becoming an artist. At eighteen, I left Connecticut and came to New York to study at Juilliard. Then I went to NYU for two years. I studied speech, diction, movement, script, text, everything related to acting. I deliberately designated four years of my life to formal training. That structure was very important for me. After college, it was just the hustle, pounding the pavement, the things that every person starting out in their profession has to go through. It's called paying your dues and having faith. First I appeared off-Broadway. Then *Coming to America* put me on the radar screen, and *ER* has completely put me on another level, an international level.

Your biggest break might not be something that translates directly into fame and fortune. Years ago, I replaced Denzel Washington when he dropped out of a movie called *Love Field.* It was an interracial love story with Michelle Pfeiffer.

There was all this buzz about "the actor who replaced Denzel." I was supposed to be the next whatever. Then, a couple of weeks later, I was fired because they thought that I was too young to play Michelle Pfeiffer's lover. At the time, I was absolutely devastated, but it made me realize then that I didn't always want to be dependent on someone hiring and firing me. That experience inspired me to go to film school so that I could become a director and have more control over my own career. Now, directing is a huge part of my life as an artist. In some ways, that was one of my biggest breaks, even though it was my most painful.

The one thing that has helped me survive is my faith. I had to get into the habit of believing in myself and of not needing other people to believe in me. I had to create this incredible, unshakable faith in myself. I've seen the evolution of my faith because it's not really just about having faith in me. It is about having faith in God—the faith that whatever I'm supposed to do, and wherever I'm supposed to be, if God wants that for me, nobody can keep me from it. Now, I still have to work as hard as I can. God helps those who help themselves, but I can only do the best that I can with the things that I control. I don't control someone hiring me, but as long as I'm working toward something good, I will end up where I need to be.

If I had to give some pragmatic advice about becoming an actor, I would say study your craft. We need to give young Black people realistic encouragement. We can encourage them by telling them, "If I really want to achieve something, I have to work hard, I've got to study, I've got to learn about whatever that desired craft is." That attitude and knowledge empower them, and it's our job to guide and encourage them. It's our responsibility to teach the youth about our past and about our present, and to help them discover the possibilities of our future.

blair underwood

If you don't have a plan, you're going to end up nowhere. We are trying to get by day by day. But if we're going to stay around year by year for our families, we have to plan for the future.

the formula for success is something I learned as a child. I got it from my parents, and I never forgot it. There are four simple rules in the formula for success. Number one: Decide what you want, set a goal. Number two: Decide what you want to give up in order to get what you want. Number three: Surround yourself with successful people. Surround yourself with the people who are doing what you aspire to do—not those who are talking about it, but those who seriously aspire to or have accomplished it—so they can show you how to do it. And number four: Plan your work and work your plan. Plan your strategy out and attack it.

You have to be very careful with advice because, as my grandfather would always say, "Check the fruit on the tree." Before you listen to someone, check the fruit on their tree. What is their area of experience and expertise? If I want to be a neurosurgeon, I'm not going to talk to a dentist. I respect the dentist, but that's not who I need to be talking to. Only listen to people who understand what your goals are. When you listen to people's advice, do it with the understanding that your script's going to be a little bit different, your life's going to be a little bit different, but you can learn from those who have gone before you. In the end, you have to have a clear a path for yourself.

There's a scene I have with Jada Pinkett in *Set It Off* when I ask about her five-year plan. That came out of an ad-lib during rehearsal because that was something I was asked all the time as a kid. Where do you see yourself in five years? If you don't have a plan, you're going to end up nowhere. So I just said that to her in a rehearsal, and the director said, "I love that, let's put that in the movie." That whole scene was about how often we don't do that. We don't think ahead, we think about the here and now, and with good reason because we are trying to get by day by day. But if we're going to stay around year by year for our families, we have to plan for the future.

I think the most important thing we can teach young people is history. To never let them forget our past. If we really instill that in them and continue to allow that history to live, then young people won't let anybody shake them or make them feel less, sub par, or second rate. It won't happen. It can't happen.

my mother was very supportive. She knew that I wanted to become an actor. When I was in high school, she read in the paper that they were auditioning for this show. And she said, "C'mon, do you really want to do this? Then I'm going to help you make your dream come true. Let's go see." You never really know if you have what it takes until you try it firsthand. So she said, "Let's see what you've got." And I walked up to the director and shook his hand firmly as my parents had taught us to do and I looked at him and told him I wanted to be an actor, and that was the beginning.

So I went to Carnegie Mellon University in Pittsburgh and studied drama there. In the middle of my third year, things got tight financially. So I went out and got my 8"x10" black-and-white head shots, and during Christmas vacation I went home and told my folks that I was moving to New York, and they said they would support me.

From Petersburg, Virginia, my mother drove me all the way to New York, in a serious blizzard, and I met an agent who sent me to *The Cosby Show*. Later, my dad and I met with Mr. Cosby, and I got a walk-on roll as Lisa Bonet's boyfriend. I just said one word, walked in the door, kissed her on the cheek, and left. I was so excited because I was on the number-one show in the country, but after that I started walking the pavement and knocking on doors and doing everything I could just to get a gig. At the same time, the show was such a phenomenon that appearing on it helped me break the ice when I went on auditions. Ultimately, the casting director from *The Cosby Show* referred me to the casting director for *Krush Groove* and that's how I got my first film role.

I was blessed from the beginning because I got about 50 or 60 percent of the roles I auditioned for, but I definitely got rejected by a lot of projects I really wanted to do. Also, there were a lot of projects where I couldn't even get in the door. As an actor, you better learn to expect and accept rejection so you can learn how to regroup and become stronger. That's why I tell young actors not to take rejection personally. It's a numbers game. You keep playing the game, you keep doing the work, keep working on your craft. Even when you're broke and nothing is coming through, treat it like it's a business, and sooner or later your number is going to come up. Don't give up, just stick to it.

i realize now that I have always used a lot of what my father calls "people politics"—being professional, looking people in the eye, giving a firm handshake, being direct. So much of that is what enables you to have longevity in this business. It's a combination of treating people the way you want to be treated and treating it as a business. My parents were always very business-oriented. They had their own business for twenty years after my father retired from the military. So we were raised with a business mentality and that's how I've kind of treated my career as well, as a business. I see myself, in this case, as a marketable commodity. You can't afford to look at yourself in any other way.

When people tell me they want to act, I try not to give too much advice. But I do tell them to be sure that you *have* to do it, that it is a need. It can't just be a desire. It cannot just be a want or a thirst. You have to believe that you have no other way to express yourself, or to feel free, or to live, if you cannot express yourself through the performing arts. Then you'll attack everything you do with a vengeance and you'll be successful. You'll be happy because you'll be able to express yourself in any medium. You won't need to be the number-one box office draw; you won't need to have the hit show on television. But if you can express yourself in an off-Broadway theater or dinner theater around the corner, you are still onstage expressing yourself. You'll be happy and that's what will make you successful.

e. lynn harris

self-acceptance

I lost everything I owned, but I found myself. I found my joy so it
didn't matter.

writing saved me. I say that all of the time. If I stopped writing, I don't think I'd
have any reason to be here. Writing did, in fact, save my life. I have never had passion like the passion I found when I started to write. Not with a book contract, not
with knowing that I have an audience, but just in the act of writing itself.

I first fell in love with writing when I was about thirty-three or thirty-four. I
started to write out of a very depressed state. I was selling computers, and I had
achieved some degree of success, but I wasn't happy. I figured I wanted to devote
the second half of my life to something that I was passionate about. I had always
written letters to my cousins when I was a kid. I got back to letter writing when a
lot of my friends started to suffer from AIDS. In these letters I would tell them stories about our friendship. I didn't want them to leave here without knowing how I
felt about them. One friend of mine, Richard Goldman, told me, "These letters
have just sustained me. You really ought to write. You really ought to tell our story.
You have a gift here. Promise me you're going to write!" I said, "Sure, Sure," but
at the time I had no idea how I could keep that promise.

By 1990, I was deeply depressed. I was not working. I had totally withdrawn and
dropped out. I really thought the world had ended. My doctor put me on medica-
tion, and I slowly started to return to the world. But I was miserable at the thought
of going back to work again in the business world. My aunt said, "Well, what do
you want to do?" I told her I wanted to write a book, and she said, "Well, you're the
only one in your way."

During that time, I saw a silly talk show that had a panel of men who fit all the stereotypes of gay men. I thought if people knew the pain involved in a life full of secrets—secrets that meant keeping so much from the people you love—they would never again be able to mock or make light of it. That's how I got the idea for *Invisible Life*. I had never written a book. I had never even written a short story, but I bought a computer and started writing. Then I started to love it, and finally, life seemed to have some joy for me.

I had no way of knowing that it was going to sell, but I had made up my mind that I wasn't going to stop until I finished this book. I lost my car. I lost everything that I had. I lost all of my possessions because they were auctioned off to pay for the storage space that I had put them in. But you know what was interesting? I didn't care. Because that was just stuff I had gotten myself. I lost everything I owned, but I found myself. I found my joy so it didn't matter. There was a time when things like that would have happened, and I would have been completely devastated. But all the things I thought I needed, I suddenly realized I didn't need at all.

When I finished, every single publisher I sent my manuscript to rejected it so I decided to publish it myself. I had a book party where I only sold forty-three copies, but in a couple of days those forty-three people were suddenly calling me saying, "I love this book! Where can I get another one to give to a friend?" Soon, I was working sixteen to eighteen hours a day because if you called me and told me you wanted a book, I would get in my car and drive it to you. Then a few angels intervened. A very conservative White guy bought my book, liked it, and gave it to an editor at Doubleday. Then one day, I was delivering the books to a bookstore and a lady saw my picture on the back. She said, "You wrote the book, but you're delivering the books, too?" I said, "I do everything," and she said, "Oh! You need an agent." She referred me to an agent, and eventually, I made a deal with Doubleday.

There are responsibilities that come with success. They are to treat people— not only your peers but people who are buying your books—with respect. When you go on tour, you have to thank people because they don't have to buy your books. They don't have to tell other people about it. I think people who've reached success with the support of the public should never forget who really pays their checks. It's not the publishing company or the record company or the film studio. It's the public. One of the most important things to me is maintaining my fan base and never letting my fans down. When I make an appearance, part of me is always thinking nobody is going to come, nobody is going to show up. When they do, I always feel so good about that. People have been so loving to me. What a tremendous blessing it is to do something that you love doing and have people respond so kindly and make you feel so successful.

I'm doing something I love, and I've reached a certain degree of success with it as well, but that is not why I write. I would like to challenge young writers to realize that writing is a craft and encourage them to work at that craft. But I also want them to realize that if they have a story burning inside of them, they owe it not only to themselves but they owe it to the world to tell that story. And you have to do it with this in mind—that only one person may read it, and that person may be your mother or you, but your writing still has value. It has value if one person reads it or if a million people read it.

Life is a gift and the way you pay back that gift is to live a full life. There have been painful episodes in my life. There have been things that I've gone through that I don't think anyone needs to go through. But I do know they made me tougher and I went through them for a reason. Life is full of disappointments and successes. Once you start believing the myths—that you can't do things because you're Black—any of those things, they become a reality. I think if you start to say this is what I want to do and I can do it and I'm not going to let any of the things that describe me keep me from doing it, it can happen. I didn't always believe that, but now I do. I know that this could all end tomorrow. But I also know that I've got the skills to turn disappointments into triumphs.

I don't think it is necessary for everyone to read what I write about, but I think if people read my books, they'll realize that they are written from the heart. I hope my work can change the way people respond when they meet someone different from themselves. When I'm gone, I would like to be remembered as a person who tried to make a difference, who tried not to change people's minds, but people's hearts.

bill t. jones

self-mastery

The toughest challenge for me was and is discipline, self-mastery.
Knowing how to not *need a person to tell you to get out of bed and go*
to the studio. Knowing how to look honestly at what you don't know.

if I could start all over again, I would still be an artist. I would still be a person
who was trying to create something provocative, informative, and mysterious.
That's what I think art is. If I make a beautiful thing, it says a lot about what I believe politically, socially. It says a lot about what it means to be a man, and a Black
man. I believe in choosing a life in the arts. If I do my art well, I think everything
important about me will be said.

I am self-defined as a maverick, a rebellious person. I never wanted to do anything the way they told me it should be done. I started dancing late in life, when I
was already nineteen, and most dancers start as children. I did not start as a classical dancer. I started as a modern dancer. Then I wanted to do strange techniques,
including improvisation. I didn't want to point my feet. I didn't want to stand at a
ballet barre. I didn't want to be in anybody's company. I rammed my head against
a lot of walls, and I burned a lot of bridges. The type of art that I do is not wildly popular because it is contemporary, avant-garde dance art.

There are times now that I wish I had been a better student. I couldn't stand to
be bored so I hopped around a lot. I wish I had sat still longer. I was a young man
who was so sure of himself because I knew that I had beauty inside of me. I knew
that if they would just let me on that stage I could turn the world on. They say a
river never turns a right angle. After it starts, it takes a long time to turn. So there
were a lot of turning points that led me to my path.

Our family worked as migrant farm workers so I was the first dancer although we all loved to entertain my parents' guests. Although I got my first taste of dancing and improvisational choreography in high school, it wasn't until I got to the university that dance became a reality, and I started to study dance seriously. I was addicted to my West African, Caribbean, and modern dance classes. A real turning point came when I did a solo piece called *Everybody Works* for a New York dance festival. The reviews described my work as "humanist, original, and extremely personal." They said no one else could have done it. That was a major epiphany. It gave me confidence and clarity. I knew that this was what I needed to be doing.

I was hungry for anything about my art. I would go to concerts, films, and read every little scrap I could about it. I was thinking all the time about my art, processing information, and developing a sensibility. It was not in a conservatory, but it was, I would say, a conservatory of life. Would I suggest that to other young people? No. It was a lot of trial and error. Go into a conservatory program. Give yourself to mentors and teachers. Learn your technique and really get your craft together.

The toughest challenge for me was and is discipline, self-mastery. Knowing how to *not* need a person to tell you to get out of bed and go to the studio. Knowing how to look honestly at what you don't know how to do and to go in pursuit of someone who can teach you, or finding a way to master a subject that you need to understand better. These things never go away. Self-mastery—in the beginning and now—is the most difficult thing, and I'd say any person worth their salt as an artist would probably concur with me on that. As you get older, and have more success, the challenge is staying aware that there is always more to learn. I say to anybody who wants to start a career, probably in anything but definitely in the arts, as you grow and have more accomplishments behind you, it's as if you are walking up an ever-increasing incline. You are carrying more and more of a burden. You've got to be stronger in your heart and in your legs because you are aging and time is against you.

Dancers and choreographers just explore movements that we all have access to, but we follow them through. As a dancer, you must be deeply in touch with your gravity, your skeleton, your muscles. Listen to natural forces. How do we stand? What happens when we shift our weight? What does it mean to let your backbone slip, to quiver and shake? What does it mean to articulate a movement? Where is the rhythm in our heartbeats and our breathing? In all of these things, if you listen to them, there is movement and beauty. As I grow older, I have to listen more carefully. I'm hungry for new frontiers of movement, but my instrument is changing. However, I don't want that to be something that diminishes my expressive powers. It should be an invitation. How can one give the indication of flying without jumping? How does an older person suggest light? It's got to be deeper and more subtle. That's where the art of dance comes from, from asking questions and trying to answer them physically.

I'm proud of the fact that I have been able to find a voice on the stage and off, but there are times when I think I cannot deal with the financial, logistical aspects. Fundraising never stops. You become exasperated. When you do a work and people don't understand it, you want to pick up your marbles and go home.

All of that fear and disappointment is not really real. What is real is the incredible rush when one is making or premiering a new work. And now that I am directing more than I dance, I see young dancers. I see their hunger and potential. I realize that this is a spiritual activity and that they are performing a vital service of encouragement just in their willingness to use their body as an instrument of joy and creativity. And I'm a part of that. That rejuvenates me. Dance is a difficult thing, and it denies you a lot, but it does give back. So here's to dance!

I believe we can all use our gifts to inspire young people. Make something. Make something beautiful, well-constructed, honest, and brave. Just do the work and make it good. Do it for the ideal audience—the young African-Americans. Smart. Tough-minded. Maybe a little wounded, but because they are young, they are predisposed to be hopeful. I always try to do something that will inspire their hope, their trust, and their own work. Every work wants to do that—to make a difference in people's lives.

I would ask young people, do you believe that you have a genius? What does it take in terms of your life, discipline, and commitment to protect that genius and to cultivate it? Because it must grow, it must be watered. It's never just a perfect thing that sits there. It has to be cultivated like a seed. Do you have the stuff to do it? I dare you to do it!

Find a way, every day, to get in touch with your movement, and get to know your body. The way you do that is to live in it with respect. Understand how to take care of a sore muscle. Don't abuse your body. Find out how to stretch, how to stand, how to feed it. What should you do? What should you eat? What should you not do? Be ferocious in your desire to work with good teachers. Keep an open mind. Don't be prejudiced. Be hungry. Absorb everything you can. So to young aspiring dancers, I say one thing—Dance! Dance every day! Dance for joy!

jackie joyner-kersee

stamina

Quitting is the easy way out. We can always find a reason not to do something. But can we gather up all the reasons why we should be doing something? I always thought that if I could better myself, it would teach me something—not just about winning, but about me.

the thought of quitting never crossed my mind. Quitting is the easy way out. We can always find a reason not to do something, but can we gather up all the reasons why we should be doing something? Can we say, "Why shouldn't I?" Everything with me was always to turn a negative into a positive. Even when I wasn't doing well or even when I wasn't winning races or people didn't know who I was, I believed eventually that I was going to get to the top.

Having a passion for what you do does not mean that success will come easy for you. If you respond to an obstacle by saying, "Oh well, this is not for me," then you have already defeated yourself. You've never really given yourself a chance. But even when you run into a bump along the way or a dead-end road, you have to believe that you can overcome it. The mind is so powerful. If you say you can, you can turn that bump into a smooth surface that leads to your goal.

For me, it wasn't about being on top or being the best in the world, it was just about improving myself. If I could just improve a tenth of a second each time I went out, I knew I was making progress. I always thought that if I could better myself, it would teach me something—not just about winning, but about me.

I never allow myself to become complacent. The reason I got better and better is that I was never satisfied. Once I broke one record, that was old news. And even though people would write that Jackie Joyner-Kersee is the world record holder, I

pushed that out of my mind because I always wanted to be hungrier and work harder. It is easy for you to get caught up in the things that are written about you and what people are saying, but then you lose sight of what got you there. The most important thing was for me to always remember what got me there, and what kept me there—working hard, listening to and learning from my coaches and my parents, and not allowing myself to change as a person or as an athlete.

I started off as a cheerleader because at the school I attended, girls could only be cheerleaders. But at a recreation center, I was introduced to basketball, soccer, and then track. That is one of the reasons that building a recreation center for young people in my hometown to replace the one that I went to has been so important to me. The first time I heard about the Olympics was when I learned about Wilma Rudolph. Wilma Rudolph was the first American woman of any race to ever win three gold medals for track in a single Olympic Games—and she was Black, too! She is an inspiration on so many different levels. She broke incredible records and set the standard for the entire world, and yet, she also made my dreams seem possible. Wilma Rudolph was a role model of mine and a mentor later on in life. But it really didn't hit home until I was actually able to watch the Olympics on television. I started to understand that I was doing the same things that those young ladies were doing, and it made me believe that I could be an Olympian, too.

It's one thing to want to be the best, but it's another to know what it takes to be the best. We have to study our own bodies and know what we are capable of doing. Your coach, or your parents, or someone else might be saying that they know you can do it, but you are the one who really knows if you can or not. You know that feeling that you get on the inside and you have to respect it and respond to it. Many times people either push themselves too hard or don't push themselves hard enough because they are not listening to their bodies and their minds. You have to protect your body and pace yourself but you cannot hold back because everything isn't perfect.

Before an event, my main goal is to stay calm. I don't expend a lot of energy worrying prior to an event because I always felt that I needed to save that energy and exert it while I was actually competing. That's true for life in general. In order to reach your goals in life, you must always move forward, put your energy into work instead of worry, and don't regret anything. I've always said to myself that whatever I do in life, I'll do it with conviction and without regret.

The most intriguing thing about the future of sports is that women are getting more and more attention and women are now starting to be marketed. I also hope we'll continue to see that the shade of your skin does not matter, that we refuse to believe that you have to have a certain image in order to sell a product. I hope that men and women of all skin colors will transcend that, and I think we all will continue to see more and more of that.

Success starts at a very young age—the habits, the behavior, and the discipline that you need are formed when you are still a child. If you have a disciplined background, you have a better understanding of why it is so important for you to do things a certain way or why it is so important to be on time. All of that translates into your school life and the other activities that you want to do. I would hope in influencing the next generation, that we influence them not only to be great athletes but to be great people—to strive to do great things and be productive citizens.

Every human being is a role model because there is always someone out there who's watching what you do and watching what you say. Fame just brings a lot of attention to entertainers, as well as athletes and other people, because we're on television. I am always aware that while I might not have an impact on the world, there may be one child out there who likes what I do and would try to emulate me. My advice to a young athlete is to be the best that you can be and surpass what I and other athletes have done. Make your own path. Be an original. Be a leader.

I would truly like to be remembered as a person who gave a lot of her time to children as well as my work. I would like people to mention my achievements in sports, the gold medals and all that, but more importantly, I would like to be remembered as a great person. That means more to me than anything in the world—that people will remember me not as one of the world's greatest athletes, but as a great person who really cared about other people.

veronica webb

struggle

*Early on in life, I realized that nothing was ever going to be handed
to me. Nothing is promised. Everything is a gift.*

i'm very willing to struggle. Struggling is actually something that I enjoy no
matter how painful it gets because that's life, and who am I not to struggle? Early
on in life, I realized that nothing was ever going to be handed to me.

At the height of your career, that is when the struggles get the hardest. That is
when the stakes are the highest. You have one day when you feel wonderful and the
next day you feel like a total complete piece of junk because the highs are really high
and the lows are really low. But I'm not a quitter. You don't get to win the Super Bowl
every year, but you've got to be in the game to get a championship ring.

I've always believed that whatever you think becomes manifest. The biggest
mistake you can make is not having clear goals. The most important thing—and
the hardest thing—is to be true to yourself.

The most important thing for me now is growing in my relationship with God.
That is something I'm working on a lot. It's easy to lose sight of faith when you live
in the material world no matter what you're doing. I think getting closer to God is
a question of becoming humble—not humble in a negative way, but humble in
the way of realizing that nothing is promised, everything is a gift. Being humble
means being thankful.

If I can do it, anybody can. I had zero background in show business. I always
loved clothes, so the first time I came to New York was on a scholarship to Otis Par-
sons School of Design. Later, I ended up going to The New School for Social Research, but I guess I thought I was majoring in hanging out, and I dropped out of

school. I was going nowhere fast. Then I was discovered by a makeup artist named Rick Gillette. He gave me a card, and I called the Better Business Bureau and checked out everything to make sure he wasn't trying to get me into some weird situation. He told me, "If you don't believe I am who I am, call *Mademoiselle* and mention my name. I do a lot of makeup for them," and I did. That is how it started.

at the beginning of my modeling career, I had no idea what I was doing. I felt very overwhelmed and was quiet as a mouse. Eventually through doing it and persevering, I started to get good at it and really enjoyed it. But it took me years and years and years to really understand what the business is—which is that you are a luxury product, no different than a Mercedes Benz or the Concord or something like that. You are meant to be hired, to be consistent. Everything about you should be in tiptop shape—your hair, your body, your nails, and your attitude.

I was astonished when I landed a cosmetics contract. I was astonished that it was actually happening, that the industry had gotten to that point where they would give that kind of contract to a Black model. I was more surprised by the industry than by myself because I worked hard. I paid a lot of dues. I didn't just stumble upon it. I arrived at it.

I'm a self-taught writer. I started writing ten years ago. All the experiences that I was exposed to and had developed in the fashion industry now goes into my work as a writer. Writing for magazines while I was modeling is part of what made modeling rewarding and bearable for me. Now, I'm getting my degree in screenwriting at UCLA. I've known that I wanted to be a writer for a long time, and it's important to me to commit to that. In 1998, I wrote my first book, *Veronica Webb Sight,* about my experiences in the fashion industry. It deals with everything I went through in this business. I wrote about my awkwardness and the feelings of self-hatred as a teenager, about getting out in the world, being dazzled by everything and getting caught up in it, and then having to come back to myself again.

You need to have your goals inside the industry, which means "I want to work for certain designers, I want to work for certain magazines, I want to make X amount of dollars." And the most important goal you need to have, the most important question is, What do you want the money for? What do you want to make of your life?

You have agents, but don't leave it up to your agents to decide that you're going to be on the cover of *Vogue* or that you're going to be in a Versace show. Tell them very clearly what you want. Tell them, "This is how I see myself. This is the kind of work I see myself doing." And then ask them, "What does it require of me to work for these clients?"

Race is always an issue. This is America. You have to realize that Black, White, Green, Purple—when you get into a business that is as subjective and competitive and exclusive as modeling, everybody you meet is going to say "No" to you when you begin. Everybody is going to say "No!" All right? And that doesn't mean that you're bad, or not good enough, or anything like that. It means that you have to earn the right to do the work.

Okay, so nobody likes your hair this season. Get a haircut. You don't fit into the clothes? Exercise and eat right. You don't know how to walk a runway well enough? Put on some high heels and practice. You can't hold still enough in a photograph? You don't have a big enough catalogue of poses that you can do? Go to yoga. Look at photography books on fashion. See how it's done. Study the industry. Study your craft.

Black models better know how to do everything they need to do to their own hair. Hair is very important to us as Black women, regardless of our profession, but for Black models your hair can have a tremendous impact on your career. That may not be fair, but that's the way it is. The entire time I worked—unless I was working with someone that I knew could do my hair—I brought every single solitary thing I needed with me, every tool, every product. I also brought shampoo and conditioner so I could wash it in case someone did my hair and screwed it up. It is extremely important to maintain that control over your body and your image.

If you live in America, you do need to come to New York in order to be a model because that is where the industry is. You have to go where the jobs are. Most importantly, you absolutely have to have an outside interest, something else that gives you pleasure that you are working on.

For a young person who wants to become a model, I would say, "Honey, get in the best shape of your life and stay in it. Have a vision for yourself and be very clear about the kind of work you want to do and why you want to do it. Enjoy absolutely every minute of it, and carry yourself like a queen."

rupaul

surrender

When I got out of my own way, all the doors opened.

wonderful things are happening all the time. Miraculous things. But if I'm not in this moment, I won't even see them. I won't even recognize them because I'm blinded by thinking about next week or something my parents did when I was a kid. Living back there in the past or living in the future makes you miss this moment. My goal is to really enjoy this moment and let the blessings move through me. Because your plan for yourself is a limited plan. It will only go as far as your brain can take it. But when you access God's plan, it is unlimited. Anything can happen.

I was a shy child, and I'm still very shy when I'm not "on." But I always knew in my gut that I would be famous because I was always singled out and scrutinized as a kid. Fame is almost second nature to me because I have always felt like an outsider. I'm used to being thought of as different. Ironically, it was the other kids in the neighborhood who informed me that I was gay. I didn't know. They somehow knew, and I was singled out because of it and because of my name, which is really RuPaul. I started my career in Atlanta at about twenty. I was in a punk rock band, and we would just do crazy music and costumes. As a joke, we all got into drag to do a performance, but when I did it people were blown away. I was, like, "What?" And they were going, "Your legs!" And I was saying, "What about my legs?" Even then I didn't think I could become famous doing that, but one thing led to another, and I started doing shows in drag. It started out as satire, a "wink," being funny. I had a character that was like a Soul Train dancer. Another one was a "Glamazon," a refined but cartoonish caricature of something that you would see in a magazine.

I had always thought that blond hair on brown skin looked outrageous. So I did all of that, and then I just capitalized on the fact that I had a great pair of sticks.

I became a local star in Atlanta, and I knew that the next step was for me to go to New York. So I moved to New York and, eventually, I became famous in the underground club scene. When I was crowned the Queen of Manhattan, I felt that that was the pinnacle of downtown superstardom. So I started really working on my music and writing, and I took the wig off. I started doing this androgynous look, but not in drag. It was definitely male. I went out and did some clubs, and nothing happened. People were, like, "That's cute, but when are you going to start doing drag again?" That's the first time I got out of God's way, and let God work His thing. In my mind, I thought that I couldn't make it in mainstream show business as a drag queen because no one had done it before. I thought I had to take the drag off, but when that didn't get a response from people, through some divine intervention, I thought, *Why not do it in drag?* And that's what I did. When I got out of my own way, all the doors opened and it was a hit. I take that philosophy with me today because who would have thought I would be famous in drag? I certainly didn't.

I've always been creative, and I have people around me who are very aggressive and know how to capitalize on all the aspects of my talents. I'm not the greatest singer, or the greatest actor, even though I work very hard at everything that I do. What I've got is personality and a loving spirit that people feel comfortable with. A loving personality is a talent that you can apply to every aspect of show business. I keep the momentum going with writing books and songs, designing clothes, and acting.

For me, training seriously as an actor means facing your past and facing your feelings. I was always afraid of emotions, afraid of the people who loved me being out of control. My parents divorced when I was seven, and they didn't explain to me what they were going through so like most children, I thought it was my fault. I still see myself as that little boy who is still trying to make heads or tails of things. Today, I'm trying to bring him up to speed. I'm saying to him, "Hey, look—none of that stuff that happened back there is your fault. And today, kid, I'm gonna take care of you. I'm gonna love you!" Now, I'm in a place where I can bring those childhood feelings up, and it's scary. But it's good because that's what people can relate to. Everybody feels the same way.

My childhood was so out of control that when I grew up, I decided I needed to control everything. I decided to take the bull by the horns. Well, if you take the bull by the horns you are bound to get hurt so now I'm just going to step back and let my higher power deal with the bull. I've missed some really beautiful blessings because I wasn't in the moment. I was too busy thinking about what happened in the past or what's going to happen in the future and not in this moment right here. I'm really working on giving up that control because I'm not running the show, God is. When I let go of that control, I can have the peace to enjoy the moment, to enjoy my life.

The toughest part has been worrying about what people thought or said about me, but now I realize that what other people think about me is none of my business. If I had listened to those people who put me down, I wouldn't be here. My mother was a real rebel. She always told me, "Do what you have to do. As long as you aren't hurting anyone else, honey, you go on and do it." Her support is the main thing that helped me to get over other people's opinions of me. I had that fire, and I know in my heart of hearts that I'm a good, kind person, that I'm not hurting anyone. People want to bring their own baggage, and their own misunderstandings. But what I'm doing is just clothes. It's just clothes and makeup. I don't want to be stifled by thinking I can't do something or by wondering what people will think. I can't live my life that way. I want to be the best I can be.

I always felt unique, like there was something different going on with me. As an adult, I realize that I'm not unique. I'm not really special because everybody feels that way. Everybody feels that everyone else got this instruction book on this life except for them. Now I realize that I'm just a human. I'm just a grain of sand on the beach, and I believe everyone has a unique quality about them. You can think, *I'm special, I'm unique, and I'm gonna make this world do what I want it to do.* Or you can accept the fact that you are just a human being, and through God's guidance, you can do what is uniquely you. That's why it's important to really know yourself. Take the time to know who you are and what you are, and then you can apply that to whatever medium you choose to work in.

It is very easy for me to separate RuPaul the entertainer from RuPaul the person because I just take the wig off. The challenge is separating RuPaul the ego from RuPaul the spiritual being. The body isn't who I really am. The body is something that will turn to dust one day. It's like a suit of clothing for my spirit. My spirit is what's real, and I have been following my spirit, and there can be nothing wrong with that. I have had to realize that most of the world is an illusion, and you cannot get caught up in illusions. I'm really trying to separate the illusions from what is real. And to me, the only real thing is the love inside of yourself, the love you give to others, and the friends you meet along the way. When I was a kid, I wanted to be famous, and I wanted to be able to create, and I have been able to achieve that. Now my wish has changed. My goal now is to really live in peace, to let the blessings flow through me and not block them.

rick fox

teamwork

The joy doesn't come in the trophy or the ring or the money. The joy comes from being part of a team, accomplishing common goals as a team, and achieving success together as a team. It's the joy of sharing something for a lifetime.

don't do it for the money. Don't play the game for commercials. Don't play it for individual successes. If you're playing it for the individual accolades, do us all a favor and play an individual sport. Because in team sports, it's got to be about the team.

In team sports, it can't be about me, and it can't be about someone else—it has to be about the team. It has to be about everybody coming together and having one shared common goal of being the best. Your individual success doesn't matter without your team. They don't ever talk about the individual who had the leading scores if his team only won twenty games. People remember teams. I have turned down a lot of money that would have put me on teams that weren't going in the right direction. For me, it was never about the money. It was about having a championship attitude and working with other individuals with championship attitudes—people who had the desire to be the best.

I first learned about teamwork from my family. I was born in Canada, but when I was two I moved to the Bahamas. When you live on a small island, there aren't too many things to distract you from the most important things that should be in any child's life—God, family, and schoolwork. For me, outside of church and family, getting an education in hopes of going to college was the focus of my life.

My mother was an Olympic athlete, and the way she was trained by her coaches influenced how she raised us. She would always challenge me to step up my game, to work even harder. Her accomplishments made me say, "Hey, I want to reach that level—to be as good as my mom." My dad was the kind of father who always told us that we could do anything. "You're a Fox, so you can do whatever you put your mind to." He had nothing but praise and was a big, loving supporter of anything we did, regardless of whether we were successful or fell on our faces. They had a kind of good cop/bad cop strategy that was very effective.

Some things were meant to happen for a reason, and my life has kind of been scripted that way—everything has fallen into place. I did not plan to go to school in the United States, but a team came down to do clinics at our high school. Two of the guys stayed at our house. They noticed my height and my athleticism, and they thought I might have the skills to become a basketball player. As a result, an Indiana high school offered me an opportunity to play basketball in the United States, and I went on to play college basketball at North Carolina.

Success is a long journey, and it is sometimes made longer by failures along the way. I have had my share of failures throughout my career. I always had this dream of being the best. That dream never goes away, but it gets harder to realize when you keep having your heart broken by basketball. There were times when I would lose faith in whether or not I'd ever be able to reach the pinnacle of success—that pinnacle meant being able to walk away, having given my life to basketball as a champion. But I kept plugging away because the dream was still there. It was still deep down inside of me. One year of basketball—even one game, one championship game—washed away all of those memories of falling short. Now I'm a champion. I'll always be able to carry that. For the rest of my life I'll be able to say, "It was all worth it because you never give up on your dream." That alone is a great reason not to give up.

All of the people I've associated with at the Los Angeles Lakers proved to be championship-caliber people in their lives on and off the court. That's the reason why we were all able to reach the highest level of success in our basketball games. In the 2000 championship season, the competition was great, but our camaraderie was greater. For me, the game of basketball returned to what it should be, which was a game you shared with teammates and players. You cared about each other. It's that same love you had when you first started playing. Basketball in high school and in college is all about the camaraderie of the team, the common goal of the team. It's not until you step into the world of professional sports that it becomes a job. What you lose sometimes in that transition is the fact that it is a game still. It is the same game that you played as a kid—the game you loved, that brought you so much joy. It's the same game that provided me with a college education, became a job that I love, and that enabled me to win a championship. All of a sudden those things come back to the forefront, and you realize that the joy doesn't come in the trophy or the ring or the money. The joy comes from being part of a team, accomplishing common goals as a team, and achieving success together as a team. It's the joy of sharing something for a lifetime. I've been rejuvenated in my love for the game. When you know what it feels like to be the best, it makes you even hungrier to go back and do it again.

The most important thing in my life is my family—spending quality time with my wife and my children. Family is the most important team in your life. I value my family, and I want them to know it. I value the support and love they give, and I want to make sure that I give them the love they deserve and that I feel for them.

I would like to be remembered as someone who was willing to do whatever it took. You can talk about wanting to be the best, but you also have to do what it takes. I was willing to leave home in the Bahamas at the age of fourteen and move to Indiana. I was willing to play college basketball in a very competitive environment. I was willing to turn down money to put myself in a position to be a champion. For me, it was about being able to make the sacrifices. And when I'm asked, "What do you want people to remember about Rick Fox and his career?" I just want them to say, "He was a team player, and he was willing to do whatever it took to win."

b. smith

tenacity

It's okay to stand on a mountain of no's in order to get to that one yes.

i've always had a lust for life! If I'm going to go to do something, I'm going to be the best I can possibly be. It's all about strength of mind, strength of body, and strength of will. To me, it's okay to stand on a mountain of no's in order to get to that one yes. I always had to knock on the door at least three times before they would let me in. I just wouldn't take no for an answer. I was always determined. When I write my autobiography, it's going to be called *It Only Looked Easy!* It was never, ever easy.

I tell people that you may not get to where you want to get the way you think you're going to get there, but I'm a believer that once you've decided what you want to do—put in 150 percent. There are endless possibilities, and I think we have to take advantage of that. You're blessed with what you grow up with. I was blessed to be 5'8", attractive with a good mind and common sense. It's more the common sense that has taken me as far as I've gotten, but I've also had to develop courage. I had to learn to be fearless.

I'm from Eveson, Pennsylvania, small town USA. The two most important role models in my life have been my parents. They were the original Martha Stewart and Bob Villa, only they were African-American and married to each other. They didn't have a lot of money, but they had incredible taste. They were very stylish, very smart, very funny, very loving, and very family-oriented. They were great entertainers and great teachers. They taught me everything about the domestic arts—how to garden, cook, restore furniture, sew, decorate, make crafts, everything. They taught me to appreciate music, art, and people. I developed a great love for entertaining

and for the home environment at a very young age. What I do today—which is lifestyle—started back then with my parents.

the first entrepreneur I met was Sally Johnson. She used to do my hair. When I was a little girl, Sally was very exciting. She had her own car. She traveled around to each small town to set up her day of doing hair, and I saw cash! I saw women give her money to do their hair and she always talked about the beauty business and beauty conventions and things like that. She was exciting, you know! This woman was independent, she made money, she traveled. She was my first business role model.

when I was in high school, I found a modeling school in the Sunday paper and convinced my parents to send me to it because my father wanted me to stop being a tomboy. By the time I graduated from high school, I had graduated from modeling school. In New York, I went to the Wilhelmina Agency, but, once again, I had to go three times.

What I learned as a model was that I was my own business. *I* was the business, and if I was going to succeed in the business, I was going to have to make sales calls, like everybody else. I remember calling *Mademoiselle,* and they would always say the same thing—to come back with new pictures, do this, do that. There was this woman who was the model editor then so I would go and see her all the time, to the point where I was making friends with the secretaries and receptionist. I had an appointment once, and when I got there the secretary said, "She's not in." I said, "But I had an appointment. Is there anyone else I can see?" She said, "Let me call the beauty department." The beauty editor looked at my book, and she booked me the next week for a beauty shoot. From the beauty shoot, they took one of the shots and made it into the cover of the July 1976 *Mademoiselle.*

I had a good career, had a lot of fun, played and worked a lot, but as I was modeling, I took dance lessons, acting lessons, singing lessons, French lessons. I read Langston Hughes and Zora Neale Hurston. I read a book that Sheilah Graham wrote. She was a mistress of F. Scott Fitzgerald, and he'd given her a list of books to read because he was her mentor so I tried to read every book on that list. I learned to set goals by reading self-help books. I was like a sponge just trying to gobble things up, trying to learn things. I was just trying to grow as much as I could.

I am an eternal student, a student of the universe. People always say to me, "You didn't graduate from college?" And I say, "No. I'm self-made."

I would write down my goals, where I wanted to go, how I thought I would get there, when I thought I'd get there, what I thought I would be. At some point I wrote down, "I think I'll go into the restaurant business." Once again, I wrote down where I wanted to go, how I wanted to get there, and when I thought I'd get there.

I started working in a restaurant at night learning the business, but I still modeled in the daytime. When people in the fashion business would come into the restaurant, they'd be stunned. "Why are you working here?" I'd answer, "Well, I'm going to open a restaurant." And they'd say, "You're crazy!" But then my restaurant *B. Smith* opened. I marketed the restaurant, I market myself, and I put that trademark *B. Smith* up there. Now thirteen years later, I have three restaurants and my own television show, *B. Smith With Style*. I even sing the theme song to my TV show!

One of the big challenges has been to maintain my integrity, build my own base, and grow into having complete control of my businesses. Often I was afraid, but I had to work through that fear. I had to make myself do things. I had to find ways to make this lifestyle work for me.

mentors are important. It's important to get in touch with someone who has great intellect that you can learn from. They don't have to be in your chosen field, but it should be somebody who you can grow and learn with. I want to have Debbie Allen's energy because when I came to New York, before I met her, she was a dancer and she had that strength and energy so I said I was going to be like her. I wanted to have Lena Horne's courage! I said I was going to be like her—elegant and beautiful and sophisticated and brave.

i think we should tell young people our stories and encourage them to understand them. We should also really push them to get the best education that they can possibly get. I was lucky and blessed because in my case, not having a formal education didn't hinder me. It could have helped because maybe I could have arrived at some of the points in my life faster. What happens when you take the time to get a formal education is that you are in a safe haven. You are able to experience life, have relationships, build friendships for life, understand disappointments, and at the same time, learn. You're a little wiser after those four years, which is why I encourage young people to go to school and enjoy it while they are there.

missy elliott

uniqueness

You have to be original and very creative to catch people's attention and hold it.

i see myself as very innovative and very creative, almost in a comic character form. My thinking is always totally different from the average person's thinking. At the beginning of my career, I was scared because I thought that people might not accept what I was doing because it was just so different from everything else that you heard on the radio. Everybody else was doing one thing, and I wanted to do something else. But I told myself, "I can't be scared. I just have to go ahead and do it."

I got past that fear when I started selling records and getting a fan base. But I still go through those times when I'm recording my album or recording a song for myself, and I'm wondering, *Are people going to accept this? Is it too far?* So sometimes I still suffer from those same worries, but I don't let them stop me from making my music.

I always remember that I started my career as a different kind of artist, and today I make sure that I maintain that difference. I make sure that I am never side-tracked by what's hot right now. In addition to the music, I have to make sure each video is totally different from everybody else's. You may be tempted or pressured to be like everybody else, but I have learned that you have to be original and very creative to catch people's attention and hold it.

Everyday life is what inspires me to write music. Going out with my friends, arguing on the phone, all of those things keep me coming up with different ideas for songs. The biggest inspiration is when my fans love what I write because they feel that I have very realistic songs. There are always songs that make people say,

"Yeah, that's what I'm talking about. That's how I feel." I maintain my originality, but there is always something in my music that people can relate to.

Even when I was a kid, I wanted to be a singer, an entertainer. I grew up in Virginia, and I started writing and singing when I was three or four. I would make up songs in my head and sing them. My mother was a singer. She was supposed to record an album and perform overseas, but she had me instead. In some ways, I am completing her dream. She has had more influence on me than any other person.

I started out in a group called Sister. We met with the members from the group Jodeci in the early 90s. One of the members, DeVante, signed us to his production company, but the record company couldn't see his vision for the group. We were just kind of caught in the crossfire. During this time, I met Puffy Combs, and he started getting me on a lot of records. He put me on an MC Lyte record and on a New Edition record. He put me on a lot of big records and helped me to get to where I am now. People started asking when I was going to come out with my own album. It meant a lot to me when fans started coming up and saying they loved the work that I did. That's what made me start saying, "Okay, people know who I am. Finally." That inspired me to produce and record my own albums.

The hardest part of this business is maintaining your success because you can be very hot one minute and not another minute. A lot of people tell you, "You're going to be like this big artist and you'll have the cars and the houses." Because we see all of that on TV, we think that's a part of the life. But it's important to understand that a lot of things you see on TV are camouflaged because once you get into the industry, you see that it's really not like that. People have told me to be very careful of what you sign, to make sure you get a good lawyer, and to not be so eager to jump into something that sounds better than it actually is. It's hard to juggle being an artist with the business side. I'm still learning. I don't know everything, but I think I'm prepared for anything. I learn something new every day.

I think it's good for a musical artist to be in either New York or Los Angeles because those are the centers of the music industry. You don't necessarily have to be in those cities to succeed because I was in Virginia when I got started. But I think New York, in particular, is a very, very valuable place to be because you run into so many artists.

Being around other artists is a good thing, especially if they're working consistently, because that inspires you to work harder. It's important to be around people who keep you motivated, but you have to be careful of the competition that can occur when people get very jealous of you. You cannot allow yourself to be distracted by what other people do and say, especially if you are a woman. The important thing for women in the industry is to feel that if they have real talent, a label will pick them up. Never sleep around because I know too many artists who do that. You have to believe in yourself, believe that your talent is real.

I don't ever get overwhelmed by the idea of being a celebrity. The only time I get excited is when I talk to a person I watched on TV who always made me say, "I want to meet them one day" or "I want to work with them." It's exciting when that actually happens so there are times when I'm, like, "Wow!" about certain people—but it's very seldom. Fame isn't the most important thing. Being true to yourself and your work is the most important thing, and ultimately the most exciting and fulfilling thing, about this business. The support of my fans and the acceptance of my music mean a lot to me, but those things don't change who I am. I'm just me. I'm just Missy every day.

cece winans

the word

*You're going to make mistakes. You're going to fall. But the important
thing is to know how to get back up and how to return to truth.*

to become a successful gospel singer, you have to have the gospel in your
heart. Being a gospel singer is more than just a talent, more than just a gift. It's
having that spirit. Singing was definitely something that God had planned for my
life. My steps were ordered.

I live the things I sing about. I don't see myself trying to be a role model, but I
try to do the right thing. I don't live the life I live because people are watching me.
I live it because I believe in what I'm singing about. I live it because God is watching me. He's watching me, and my goal is to see Him face to face. I'm going to live
the same way whether I'm in or out of the spotlight.

My one prayer for my children is that they will love God with all their heart,
soul, and mind because I know as an adult that those teachings never leave you
no matter what country you're in, no matter what company you're in. You always
hear those teachings. You try to act like you don't sometimes, but I don't care how
loud the music is—you hear the word. And when you do mess up, you know how
to get back. That's the thing I love about life. Even though you go through your
ups and downs and challenges, if you persevere, if you keep going, you're going
to come out a better person. None of us likes to experience pain, but through pain
you grow. Through pain you mature, you learn. You're going to make mistakes.
You're going to fall, but the important thing is to know how to get back up and
how to return to truth.

i've been singing all my life in the church and at home. I have seven older brothers and two younger sisters, and we are a family of singers so we always had competition. We gave out awards. We dogged you if you were horrible. But it was always a healthy competition. Even to this day, we're each other's greatest critics and greatest fans.

I sang my first solo when I was about eight years old. Sister Glen supervised the kids' choir, and she had arranged it with my parents. I had no say so at all, and nothing could get me out of it. My first solo was "Fill My Cup, Lord." Recently, I recorded an *a cappella* version of it just as I sang it as a child.

Now that I look back, even in my first solo, I felt something that was more than just singing. I felt something in the response of the people that was much bigger than I was. I knew that it was a calling, that it was God's spirit, His direction. But His plan for my life came later, when I was about seventeen.

My first break was with the PTL Club. BeBe and I became a part of the PTL ministries. We definitely got our training singing into the television camera. You're reaching more people that you ever dreamed of, all at the same time. So every performance on camera becomes more and more important because you realize that it's the largest possible audience, much more than a live audience. Captivating an audience is something you really have to learn to do. You have to be relaxed in front of the camera and draw people in. At the time, it seems like it's just a camera. But then when you go out, you realize so many thousands of people have seen you. You discover the power of a camera. You discover the power of television.

Once they saw us, the TV viewing audience started asking us to come to their churches and sing. Then we started getting offers from record labels, and we signed with Sparrow Records, which was strictly a Christian label. After we recorded our album, they took it over to Capitol Records, and Capitol wanted to sign us with the album just the way it was. They didn't ask us to change anything. They loved what we did, and that's how we really got introduced to the world.

i was prepared creatively to be a professional gospel singer. I was prepared vocally. But as far as the business, I definitely was not prepared when I went in, but you become prepared quickly once you're thrown in and you have to learn. When I was in church, I was just singing. I was just doing what I know God had called me to do. You do the same thing in the studio, but you have the whole business that's connected with it.

One of the things that I definitely stress to new artists is that you should learn the business inside and out. Whoever you are, whatever you want to go into, you should really learn what you're about to become or what you're about to be involved in. You always have to go through things but you don't have to go through a lot of the unnecessary disappointments in your career if you prepare, if you really research what you want to do.

you have to have confidence. If you don't have confidence in yourself, nobody else will. The more I sang in front of other people, the easier it became. I still feel the butterflies before I sing, but I found out that's not always a bad thing. That's a good thing.

the biggest challenge for me today is balancing everything. It's a constant challenge to keep everything going. I'm a wife, a mother, an artist, and I just started a record label. Just keeping everything balanced can be difficult. You can get overwhelmed. God's presence and His word keep me from staying overwhelmed and keep me focused on my purpose and why I do what I do. Keeping peace of mind is more important than anything. Money doesn't buy you happiness. It'll pay the bills, but it's not the answer to your heart, and your mind, and your spirit. That only comes from God's word.

the most important thing about being a singer is being able to relate what you feel to others, to touch them. A singing style is something that you just have. You just feel it. We're so much more alike than we are different. A lot of us who come from the Black community, church community, were raised the same way. Everybody has a different definition of success, and my definition comes from the way I was raised. To me, success is being happy. Success is being yourself. Being comfortable with yourself, with who you are. And I owe all of that to my upbringing. You have a lot of people who make money and reach a goal but are unhappy or not enjoying what they do and to me, that's not success. Success is being well balanced and having your priorities straight. Keeping things in perspective. Knowing what's important, what's not important, and how important family is, how important it is to be a good parent, to be a good spouse. Because those are the things that last. Those are the things that count. It's true especially if you have children because they grow so quickly so every moment is important. Those moments are the most important things. Creating moments. Memory moments.

acknowledgments

First, I give thanks to God for blessing me, and giving me the vision, talent, and gift of creativity. *Thank you for watching over me each and every day of my life, but especially during the writing and production of this book. Thank you, Father, for a supportive family and wonderful friends who were by my side throughout not only this project but throughout my life. Thank you, Father!*

To my distinguished parents, Mr. Jordan Smith and Mrs. Eunice Smith, thank you for always believing in me, especially during those teen years when I must have certainly drove you both gray. I love you with all my heart. Thank you for showing me, through your example, how to love and stay in love! I pray to one day share the love and friendship that you both have shared for over forty years.

To Vanessa Williams, one of the most beautiful women on the planet, thank you for writing such an amazing introduction and for believing in my project from the very beginning. Your words are as timeless as your beauty.

To each of my fifty participants, their agents, managers, and publicists, thank you for sharing a bit of your life experiences with me and for making this project truly amazing.

To my anchor, Tanya McKinnon, literary agent extraordinaire, thank you for understanding my project and for making it the best it could be. I also thank you for understanding my vision and bringing the perfect chefs to the kitchen to help me prepare the perfect meal. Dinner is finally ready to be served.

To my writer, Dionne Bennett, you are truly a blessing. I have fallen in love with the magic you have brought to these pages. Thank you for losing sleep in the name of *Sepia Dreams*.

To my wonderful editor, Heather Jackson-Silverman, thank you for all your hard work in turning my dream into reality. You have helped to make *Sepia Dreams* the best it can be. Thank you also to the entire St. Martin's Press staff who worked hard in the name of *Sepia Dreams*. Designers Shea Kornblum and Victoria Kuskowski, and the publicity team of Gregg Sullivan and John Murphy. Thank you.

To my project coordinators, Nicole Williams and Darlene Gillard, who spent many stressful hours helping me produce the photo shoots and arrange interviews. Thank you! Without you this would still be a dream. I cannot thank you enough.

To my photo agent, Lewis Van Arman, and the cast of LVA, Audra Alexxi Jones, Ruth Geyer, and Maria Cutrona, thanks for your undying devotion, admiration, patience, and support throughout my project.

To Lloyd Boston, my man of color, thank you for all your support and advice in bringing *Sepia Dreams* to life. To Malika McKee and Latika Russell, thank you for staying up all night to define "the look" of *Sepia Dreams*!

To Delora E. Jones, and the entire cast of transcribers who worked on *Sepia Dreams*, thank you for all your hard work and support on this project. A Steno Service, Tshinguta Lily Lufuluabo, Linda Skinner, Linda Taylor, Corine Griffith, Paulette Brown, Gayle Williams, Claudia Bibb, Sadye Fristo, Kathryn Daniels, Diane L. Moss, Bob Meadows, and Monica Norton.

To Shawn and Wayne Bryant at Gameface Ventures, thank you for getting the *Sepia Dreams* Web site up and running, and for bringing the perfect sponsors on board. Also thanks to Barry at Artmandu Media for designing an amazing site for all the world to see.

Thank you to my creative support teams in New York and Los Angeles. The studios and studio managers, the many hair stylists, makeup artists, wardrobe stylists, and photo assistants who worked or donated space because they believed in my vision. Sam Fine, Oscar James, Laura Mulberg, Barry White, Myla Moralas, Derrick Ruthledge, Christopher Michaels, Greg Brockington, David del La Cruz, Tamara Otto, Wendy Nelson, Liza Mae Nettles, Justi Embree, Natalie Dixion, Sharon Miller, Ms. Mei Tao, Crush Boone, Jeff Tautrim, Jimmy Fishbine, Scott Quinn, Brisco Savoy, Lenora Kim, Chris Spiridigliozzi, John Collazo, Douglas McMahon, Jesse James Halpern, Nat Norwood, Marcus Guillard, Trina Cooper, Kenny Hammond, Ronnie Thomas, Stephanie Willis, Sun Studios, Milk Studios, John, Paul, and Dave Baker at Fifth & Sunset LA studios, Caroline at Spot Studios, LA Lofts Studios, and the entire *Men of Color* crew.

A very special thank you to the Crystal Agency in LA who provided hair, makeup, stylist, and manicurist all in the name of *Sepia Dreams*. Thank you, Crystal Wright and Maleeza Korley, for all your support throughout the entire project.

My deepest appreciation to my family, friends, peers, and clients who helped, inspired, and supported me during the making of *Sepia Dreams*. To my sisters Veronica Davis and Donna Jenkins; my brothers-in-law, Greg and Mark; and to my wonderful nephews and niece, Shane, Shantel, Sterling, and Lyric, never stop dreaming and reaching for your goals. Thanks to all my former students at SVA—remember, "always shoot what you love." To my creative New York family, Sam Fine, Martin Cooper, Karen Shu, Scott Sillers, Lloyd Boston, Gail O'Neill, thank you for all your input and devotion to my project. Also a special thanks to Wanakee Pugh, Felicia Carte, Sarah Irby, Hemali Dassani, Cheryle Free, Marcia Griffith, Nicole Robinson, Boris Kodjoe, Kwaku Alston, Cynthia Bailey, Leon Robinson, Rosie Tenison, Renee Tenison, John Faulkner, Pauline Pursard, Aria Das, Dion Bray, Terry McMillan, E. Lynn Harris, LaTonya R. Jackson, Beverly Peele,

Gerard Harris, Antoinette Price, Glenna Scruggs, Deborah Gregory, Deardra Matthews, Pearl Harb, Bernedette Beekman, Gary Dourdan, Susan Garrison, Sidney Poitier, Amen Ra Productions, Justine Ha, Lori Davis, Wesley Snipes, Lucy Goncalves, Nicky Norris, Jean Gilles, Jane Bond, Adele Hall, Kim Holmes, and Ronette Calhoun-Scott. To my good friend Allen Edmond, who pushed me to leave South Carolina in pursuit of my dreams. Thank you all.

My heartfelt gratitude goes out to the many publicists, agents, managers who helped in turning my dream into a reality. Gena Avery, Marla Weinstein, Jennifer Hollina and Allen Eichhorn, Joelle Pezely, Malinda Dancil, Gwendolyn Quinn, Kevin Gasser, Lorraine for Iman, Cheryle Fox Spencer, Chandra Brooks, Lee Wallman, Charlie Fox, Debra Parker, Wilma Remy, LaVon Leek-Wilks, Grace for B. Smith, Simone Reyes, Lita Richardson, Sloan Wells, Marita Stavoro Miller, Cathy Jordan, Lorraine Smith, Hazel for Patti LaBelle, Pearl at Elite Sports Marketing, Carl Nilsson, Bjorn Amelan, Lenord, Elie Selden, Iola, Camille Troy, Carol, Akina Rohmann, Jamike Pinede, Bernard Jacobs, Evan Haney, JoAnne for Mr. Parks, Diane Martin, Rose, and the entire de Passe Entertainment family, Lisa at Tommycat Productions, Bethann Hardison, Christine, Karen for Debbie Allen, Kezia Collins, Janine Fox, Chocolate Swan Productions, Arnold Robinson, Jakki Taylor, Debra at Bankable, Chris Chanbers, Justin Ha, Lori Davis, Amen Ra, Tracey Kimble at HBO, Lianne, Rodney Peete, Guy Troupes, Ché Graham, Jay Manuel, and the entire Lux imaging family. Thank you for all the hard work you put into *Sepia Dreams*. Thank you all.

To my brothers, Leon Robinson, Boris Kodjoe, Eriq La Salle, Kwaku Alston, Gerard Harris, Martin Cooper, Scott Sillers and Same Fine. Thank you, fellas.

To the true love of my life, Saila Sattar, thank you for being by my side with support and understanding and for bringing peace, love, and happiness into my life. From the depths of my soul, I love you.

Someone once said, "One man's fantasy is another man's job." I have been truly blessed that I live my fantasy every day through my job. However, my job could not happen without the many people who work behind the scenes to make the magic happen. To all of you who's name I have mentioned and any who I may have overlooked, thank you for helping me make my dream come true.

—*matthew jordan smith*